A word to the readers

We do not know what is happening to us, and this is precisely what is happening to us, not to know what is happening to us
José Ortega y Gasset

Human today has fallen into a terrible fire, which is called Alienation. Self-forgetfulness causes human to give up loving himself and not discover a reason for his existence. When he cannot discover the cause of his own existence, at certain moments he engages in actions that are often unintentionally anti-human. He does not know what action he is taking and he does not know whether this action was right or wrong in a situation where society has led human to depoliticize. He only acts and finds no reason for his actions. With a logic that considers truth dead and completely relativistic, that person will be more likely to justify his actions and will not seek the truth at all, or anything close to the truth. Human will not understand himself until he seeks to discover the closest thing to the truth, and human who does not know his individual identity will have no understanding of collective identity and Otherness. There is a close relationship between identity and truth. Without identity, there is no truth, and where there is no truth, anonymity shows itself.

The way forward for human is to think about the self. By looking at history, by taking refuge in art, by understanding philosophy, by perusing mythology and cultures, human can see his true face in the mirror and visualize another in the mirror.

The aim of Hermes Magazine is to present beauty and glory to its audience in the form of words, and by publishing the different ideas of writers from different countries and cultures, to some extent represent the true nature of human societies. We are very happy that you are the reader of this magazine and you are following us.

YOUR FRIEND,

Mohammad Abedi

Contents

Art History

Other Articles

Poetry

Short Story

PHILOSOPHY

MAKING HISTORY THROUGH SUBALTERNITY: THE APPLICATION OF THE GRAMSCIAN PERSPECTIVE IN THE INDIAN CONTEXT

BY DIEGO LAUDATO

<< The working class will have to be called upon and told that it must lead India's democratic revolution and the working class will have to carry out this task by providing leadership to the struggle of its most firm ally, the peasantry. So, it is the responsibility of the working class to organise the peasant movement and raise it to the stage of armed struggle. The vanguard of the working class will have to go to the villages to participate in armed struggle. This is the main task of the working class [...]. >> [1].

Charu Mazumdar, also known as Charu Majumdar, had been a major figure in the Indian communist tradition, particularly committed with proselytism and indoctrination of Maoist theories among Indian peasants. He's mainly remembered because of his involvement in the 1969's Naxalite movement, of which he is considered the very founding father. The term "Naxalite" derives from the West Bengal's village of Naxalbari, where the uprising firstly broke out in 1967. The conflict was carried out by the Communist Party of India (Marxist) against the Indian government. Main goals of the rebellion were the improvement of the land rights and of the agricultural workers. Majumdar, one of the Party leaders, also defined the political pattern of the group by means of a collection of writings then named "Historic Eight Documents", the last of which is the text from which the introductory pas- sage of this essay has been extracted. These papers became in a sense the Naxalites' manifesto, laying the foundations for their concrete revolutionary activity.

As it can be observed by the texts, Majumdar's way to establish Communism was based on the role of peasantry in the armed struggle. He was actually well aware of the Indian peculiar context. Latter's social conditions demanded indeed for very different political and military tactics than the ones carried out during the Russian October Revolution[2]. In the first decades after World War II, the Indian subcontinent for the most part was not at all an industrialized country. Rather, it was a predominantly agricultural context, in which peasantry represented the majority of the population. The agrarian revolution was, therefore, the very imminent target for Indian communists of the time. In this sense, Chinese Revolution[3] and its leader Mao Zedong were much more influential points of reference than the Soviet model for the revolution's success. The

Majumdar's path toward the establishment of a communist society in India involved the indoctrination of the working class by the Party's cadres. Aware of both the Chinese experience and of the local context, they should had avoided an isolated guerrilla. Rather, they should had looked at the achievement of a leading role among peasantry in order to help the latter to develop a proper class-consciousness, through which it could eventually rose up against the bourgeois elite side by side[4].

The point of a class struggle in which the proletariat would led peasants toward revolution finds a major reference in Antonio Gramsci's thought. Gramsci has been one of the most important heterodox Marxist of the 20th century. He investigated the possibility of success of a communist revolution in an almost completely agrarian contexts. For this reason, already before Majumdar, Gramsci focused on the nature of peasantry as a social class. According to him, in particular, peasants are a proper living force, with their own political, cultural and social dimension. Nevertheless, even where they are the numerical majority of people, they are always a in status of sub- ordination to the dominant classes. Precisely as stated almost half-century after by Majumdar, Gramsci as well did not minimize the working class's role in the class struggle even in rural areas. In facts, he insisted on the former's leading attitude within the patterns of the revolution. According to him, indeed, the only way to successfully overturn capitalism was the creation of a proper alliance which mobilized the entire mass of workers, tying together both the proletariat and the peasantry against the capitalist dominion. Gramsci's heterodoxy in this case was represented by his interest in promoting peasantry to a proper class, which could eventually achieved, through an articulated process of development of an own consciousness, its revolutionary attitude. In this way therefore, communist revolution was no longer considered as an exclusively proletariat's prerogative. It should resulted rather from the arranged efforts of both peasants and industrial workers, which in this sense merged together in shaping a wider and more comprehensive class of workers. In Gramscian perspective, such broadened group is identified by the concept of subalternity. This term actually points out a slightly different understanding of that system of power relations generally outlined in Marxist narratives.

Rather than focus on the mainstream clash between the working class and the capitalist, the Italian philosopher in facts suggested to look at both peasantry and proletariat as a single social class. The same happened for the group opposed to the "subalterns", as he labeled this new social class. No longer addressing the struggle only toward factories' owners, he actually identified a wider group of capitalists, composed by the sum of all those who hold every kind of means of production. The name he found for this enemy faction was superordinates. In those contexts like the Indian ones in which there was not a full-developed industrial society, this kind of binary opposition between subalterns and superordinates could actually depict in a more precise way the patterns of a society in which the clash between peasants and landowners actually has greater importance than the one between proletarians and factories' owners[5].

According to this, the path toward Communism suggested by Gramsci seems to be almost the same one outlined by Majumdar in his "Historic Eight Documents". Not by chances, Naxalite movement developed in West Bengal, an Indian region whose economy has always been exclusively based on agriculture. The focus over peasants was in this regards unavoidable, as well as the strong Maoist attitude of the group. The Chinese Revolution was indicated indeed as the suitable example of a successful communist revolution in an agrarian context. In particular landless and poor peasants were identified by Majumdar as the most revolutionary component of that society and therefore the most obvious ally for industrial workers in order to establish an unified formation of subalterns operating against capitalist forces[6].

The application of the concept of subalternity in India, nevertheless, did not exhaust its potentiality in the Naxalbari's uprisings. Actually, it has resulted in other major implications in this context, which seems to be actually an interesting laboratory of investigation for this matter. This part of the world has been, indeed, the birthplace of one of the most important trend of contemporary historiography, i.e. the Subaltern Studies. Such research line was founded by a prominent Indian intellectual, Ranajit Guha, who at the end of the Seventies started an academic conversation with a group of other compatriots, all of them based in Great Britain. The group is considered one of the most influential tendency within the wider academic branch of Postcolonialism. Their approach was one of history from below, according to which the investigative focus was finally shifted from the elites to the popular masses. In this sense, both Gramscian concept of subalternity and the Naxalite's experience represented pivotal premises to the development of the Subaltern Studies group.

In particular Guha oriented the group's discussion in the production of an unusual historical perspective aimed to insert a completely new subject within the mainstream Indian historiography. This new actor was represented exactly by the peasantry. In particular the academic group focused on the role that this specific social class achieved in the process of Indian national independence. Until that moment, indeed, a strong elitist approach had been largely dominant in the reconstruction of the Indian history, resulting in a partial interpretation of the events in which peasants, that were the great majority of the population, disappeared by official records in favor of the national elite's exaltation. In order to react to this partisan void, Guha and the others deepened the relation between mass struggles and the revolutionary theory, applying in this sense Gramsci's reasoning about subalternity to the peculiarity of Indian context[7].

An emblematic self-analysis of the Subaltern Studies' contribution has been made by one of his most renowned spokesman, i.e. Dipesh Chakrabarty. Chakrabarty investigates the inclusion of subaltern pasts in the historical narrative. According to him, this is a process carried out by "democratically minded historians" who avoid the omission from the mainstream ac- counts of what he labeled as "minorityhistories". Included in this group are chronicles of all those social classes such as women, indigenous people, children, the elderly and also the working-class and the peasantry. Nevertheless, Chakrabarty goes beyond this point. He states, indeed, that such "minority histories" are not just the ones related to proper groups of subalterns.Actually, they can be found even among the reports concerning dominant classes. Among the mainstream narrations of the elites, indeed, there are minor historical reports which stand in the background, not participating in the major historiography. This is the very assumption of the telling difference that he stresses: rather than limiting the investigation on the past of subaltern people, "minority histories" are actually able to show a wider categorywhich includes the whole amountof what he calls "subaltern pasts". He proceeds then analyzing a typical instance of a subaltern past, already investigated by his masterRanajit Guha: the1855's Santhal rebellion.The Santhal rebellion occurred in the present-day region of Jharkhand. Lasted between June 30th 1855 to January 3rd 1856, the revolt was organized by the Murmu Brothers. According to the conventional chronicles, they led the Santhal population against both the British colonial entity and the local collaborationist rulers. Main goal was to end the unsustainable duty sys- tem held by the East India Company's officials and Indian authorities' joke. In spite of the way in which the episode has been narrated by mainstream historiography, which highlighted the economic and social reasons, in this specific account insurgents' consciousness is presented as the very pillar of the rebellion[8]. Guha indeed reinterpreted this historical event focusing on the influence that the insurgents' consciousness had on the broke out of the rebellion[9].

This line of research seems actually to be quite consistent with one of the most important Chakrabarty's assumption, that is the well-known difference between "History 1 " and "Histories 2s". According to the author "History 1 " concerns that major chronicle whose events are completely included within the typical capitalist dynamics. Quite clearly, this dominant category naturally tends to be included into the mainstream historiography. On the other hand, "History 2s", which not by chances is written in a plural form, do not emerge from the labour-capital conflict. Rather, in this different historical perspective people's private dimension becomes the very main character. The narrations belonging to this second group concern indeed that kind of private awareness which is still part of the story, with its own contribution to the course of times, though nevertheless it does not take any part within the official records[10].

Eventually, this last point opens a completely new perspective, through which the Subaltern Studies group has been able to challenge one of the most important feature of the Western historiography, i.e. secularization. The presence of divine entities, as well as the very God's agency in history, have been always negated in the framework of the mainstream chronicle, or "History 1 ". Rather, they found an interesting compatibility in the "History 2s" ' context, in which this kind of limitations is avoided. Through a deep understanding of this category indeed, non-materialistic patterns are properly included within its ranks. With this in mind, Chakrabarty develops his own interpretation of the Santhal uprising. Briefly outlining, according to him a major role was indeed achieved by the statement of a rebel. He reported the appearance of the god Thakur, who explicitly told him to revolt against the established order. In this reconstruction, therefore, the divine element acquires an own role in the story. Indeed the supernatural here goes through a process of anthropologization occurred by means of the experience narrated by the rebel. Through his words it acquires therefore an own agency. It actually did have its value in the following events, whose consequences cannot be neglected in the historiographic report of the episode[11].

This interpretation eventually seems to close the circle of this paper. Its peculiar anti-secular attitude, indeed, finds a very emblematic reference in the forerunner of Subaltern Studies, i.e. Gramsci and his heterodox Marxism. The Italian communist, indeed, already in the first half of the 20th century and in a Western country, explicitly claimed to not underplay the role of religion among subaltern classes, as it was in facts typical in the Marxist tradition of atheism. Rather, he pointed out the pivotal importance of the supernatural element in the peasant culture. According to him, it actually provided peasants of the general framework for real political activity[12]. Both these authors have understood the impossibility for historians to accept this value of this category according to the mainstream framework of the historical analysis. Nevertheless, they both have acquired the awareness that the supernatural, directly or anthropologized, informs the course of time, prompting people in acting according to its patterns. This is the case of a those subaltern pasts included in the History 2s's reports: something that cannot be accounted in History 1's, nevertheless, through people's private dimension, has its own agency in making history.

References

[1]   David Arnold, Gramsci and Peasant Subalternity in India, in Vinayak Chaturvedi, Mapping Subaltern Studies and the Postcolonial, Verso, 2000, London, pp. 24-49.

[2]   Dipesh Chakrabarty, Provincializing Europe. Postcolonial thought and historical difference, Princeton University Press, Princeton, 2008.

[3]   Ranajit Guha, The Prose of Counter-Insurgency, in Ranajit Guha and Gayatri Chakravorty Spivak, Selected Subaltern Studies, Oxford Univer- sity Press, New York, 1988.

Webliography

[4] Charu Mazumdar, Carry Forward The Peasant Struggle by Fighting Re- visionism, in Charu Mazumdar Reference Online Archive , April, 2004, https://www.marxists.org/reference/archive/mazumdar/1966/x01/x02.htm , last view: 23/10/2021.

Endnotes

[1] C. Mazumdar, Carry Forward The Peasant Struggle by Fighting Revisionism, in Charu Mazumdar Reference Online Archive, April, 2004¬:
https://www.marxists.org/reference/archive/mazumdar/1966/x01/x02.htm, last view: 23/10/2021.

[2] The October Revolution is the name through which historians are used to refer to the last part of the Russian Revolution, which in 1917 led Bolsheviks to get the power in the region, establishing the first Communist society in history.

[3] The Chinese Communist Revolution in turns indicates the civil conflicts which led the Chinese Communist Party and its Chairman Mao Zedong to proclaim People's Republic of China on 1st October 1949. In spite of its Russian precedent, the Chinese case was characterized by a much more marked agrarian nature.

[4] Ibidem.

[5] D. Arnold, Gramsci and Peasant Subalternity in India, in V. Chaturvedi, Mapping Subaltern Studies and the Postocolonial, Verso, 2000, London, pp. 25-34.

[6] C. Mazumdar, Carry Forward The Peasant Struggle by Fighting Revisionism, op. cit.

[7] D. Arnold, Gramsci and Peasant Subalternity, op. cit., pp. 24-25.

[8] D. Chakrabarty, Provincializing Europe. Postcolonial thought and historical difference, Princeton University Press, Princeton, 2008, pp. 97-102.

[9] R. Guha, The Prose of Counter-Insurgency, in R. Guha and G.C. Spivak, Selected Subaltern Studies, Oxford University Press, New York, 1988.

[10] D. Chakrabarty, Provincializing Europe, op. cit., p. XVII.

[11] Ivi, pp. 102-106.

[12] D. Arnold, Gramsci and Paesant Subalternity in India, op. cit., p. 32.

AFRICAN PHILOSOPHY: THE IMPACT OF PROVERBS AND FOLKTALES ON AFRICAN CULTURE

BY LAURA ADEWOLE

Abstract

There is a general misconception by the Western world that Africans were largely illiterate, ignorant, and barbaric. Some Western scholars who hide behind the word 'primitive' to categorize African people often admit that African people have culture and traditions but refuse to recognize the people's history, religion, and even their philosophy.

However, this is not the case because just as other continents in the world, Africans are deeply rooted in values and the wellbeing of their culture. Some sources of African Culture include Religion, myths, superstition, Proverbs, Folktales among others.

This article looks at African philosophy and the impact of proverbs and folktales on African Culture.

Introduction

The existence of African Oral literature is evident in the Proverbs and folktales of Africans. These proverbs and folktales are used to teach lessons about life. They offer wisdom, depth, truth as well as the discovery of ideas.

Proverbs and folktales are some of the ways Africans preserved their culture and educated themselves and their young ones. In many African Countries, Proverbs and Folktales are used in molding characters, to enhance modern life, create positive influence and teach moral values like good character, integrity, humility, courage, honesty, and unity.

The main objective of this paper is to examine the impact of proverbs and folktales on African Culture.

African Philosophy

The word 'Africa' can be traced to the Latin adjective "aprica", which means sunny. 'Africa' is used to denote the land of sunshine, of the black race, and mostly refers to the sub-Saharan regions of

Negroes[1]. The Continent of Africa consists of 54 (fifty-four) internationally recognized countries with different tribes and unique cultures and traditions. It is the world's second-largest and second-most-populous continent.

To understand what African Philosophy is, we need to understand the history of the intellectual processes and ideas generated in Africa, the culture, history, and experience of the people, to appreciate and connect to the African intellectual explanation and reality of existence[2].

The one of hallmarks of African Philosophy is morality. You can either be good or bad. When one is found evil, he or she is punished and/or ostracized from the community. The values and rules that bind the poor to the community also bind the rich. It must be noted right from the outset that a substantial number of Sub-Saharan African languages do not have words that can be said to be direct equivalents of the word 'ethics' or 'morality'[3]. The closest word which can be interpreted in some local languages is 'Character'. For example, In the Yoruba language[4], the word 'iwa' means both character and morality. Another example is the Akan language[5]; where a speaker wants to say, "He has no morals", or, "He is immoral", or "He is unethical", "His conduct is unethical", he would almost invariably say, "He has no character" (Onni suban)[6].

Another hallmark of African philosophy is its values. The concept of African values does not convey only one meaning. Hence, the use of African values could mean different things to different people such as: African values as common values that belong to all African cultures without exception, as in the case of pan-African values. African values as values found within a particular African culture or values from any African tribal culture, like the Igbo, the Yoruba, the Hausa, etc. African values as values that belong to an African, as personal values[7].

Culture is also an important hallmark of African Philosophy. Culture is often seen as the total of the peculiarities shared by a people[8]. It is the totality of the way of life evolved by a people in their attempts to meet the challenge of living in their environment, which gives order and meaning to their social, political, economic, aesthetic and religious norms thus distinguishing a people from their neighbors[9]. In an African society, apart from proverbs, and folktales, language, religion, values, dance, myths, superstitions, mode of dressing, and so on makeup African culture. These lists vary from African societies. The culture of a people sets them apart from other human societies.

Although African traditions were largely unwritten, they have found ways to pass and preserve their traditions to other generations.

Proverbs

Proverbs or as popularly called wise sayings are words of wisdom passed down from one generation to the next. The wisdom contained in these proverbs is universal and appreciated all over the world. Although they vary from one language to the other and are influenced by societal values and ethics, they achieve the same purpose and meaning.

Proverbs are based on symbolic or metaphorical language. Metaphors used as an aspect of a teaching method could be effective because they could enhance the conceptualization of abstract ideas[10]. Proverb is a way by which the society warns its members of the dangers of life[11].

The Yorubas of Nigeria cleverly emphasize the worth of proverbs with a proverb of their own, by saying, "A proverb is a horse that can carry one swiftly to the discovery of ideas."[12]. Another famous example that has spanned the globe appearing in American movies and books is the Nigerian proverb "It takes a village to raise a child."[13]. and the Zulu proverb; "You cannot chase two antelope at once."

Like Folktales, proverbs also encode the traditional settings of the African and their belief system. Nguni[14] proverb "Motho ke motho ka motho yo mongwe" (meaning "A person is a person through others") is a description of the African way of life[15].

In Fagunwa's novel, Wole Soyinka thus translate several of Yoruba proverbs like "When our masquerade dances well, our heads swell and do a spin", "The goods which he truly understands are what a trader sells"; "He who must do what no one has done before him will experience what no man has experienced before".

Most African writers have used proverbs to enrich their novels. These authors have employed these forms as a medium to encourage and inspire Africans, especially the new generation who have turned away from their roots and allowed the African tradition to be relegated to the background, asking them to return to their roots and forfeit the Western ways[16].

The translation of African Proverbs makes it relatable and easy to see the intelligence and life experiences African people possess. People with different cultures, beliefs, and traditions have many proverbs in the same context. Some of these proverbs from other continents have their equivalent meaning in Africa. For example, the French saying "Qui vole un oeuf vole un boeuf" meaning "He who steals eggs steals cattle," is also familiar to the American proverb "Give him an inch and he will take a mile.

Folktale

Folktale is defined as a characteristically anonymous, timeless, and placeless tale circulated orally among a people[17]. Folktale is a form of oral literature passed from one generation to the other. They contain stories that teach moral lessons, some contain riddles, myths, super. Folktales, as a form of oral literature, draw their material from the realities of society and hence reflect people's values and worldview. It opens a window of understanding to social norms, values, ideas, and culture.

Some of these stories have been a source of influence for African drama, prose and poetry. One interesting thing about Folktales is that some of these stories can and have been modified to fit certain purposes to conform to the changing society's contemporary experience, ideas, and values. Some writers have argued that Africa had relegated their traditional folktales and have replaced them with western culture due to colonialism and globalization. However, the narrative that African writers or Africans themselves have neglected the tradition and practices that make up their culture is false. Africans have found ways to preserve their folktales. One of which was infusing these folktales in creating works of literature. Prominent African Writers like Chinua Achebe, Chimamanda Ngozi Adichie, Wole Soyinka, Ayi Kwei Armah, Mariama Bâ, Nadine Gordimer, Ngugi wa Thiong'o have drawn their source of inspiration from African folktales and projected African Art and beauty in their works[18].

No literary writer can boast of composing a piece of work solely from his thoughts and ideas. Every writer is a member of society and his society influences him consciously or unconsciously[18]. This is seen through their writing where the writer draws its source of inspiration. Where such is published in the same society the writer is influenced by, it becomes relatable to the readers of that society.

The narration of folktales in the early days usually starts around a fire with an elderly person as the anchor and surrounded by little children. For example in the Yoruba culture, the elderly person starts the chants "Alo o" (Story) and the children reply "Alo". The elderly person goes ahead to tell them a story and the inquisitive children pay attention. This depicts how folktales are passed from the old generation to the new generation. Folktales can also be likened to bedtime stories parents tell their children to lull them to sleep.

In African folktales, Objects like spoons, wood, and so on; Animals like the tortoise, Lion and so on and nature, take on human characteristics such as greed, honesty, and integrity to teach moral lessons. For example, slow Animals like Tortoises and snails are usually used to portray patience or to discourage deceit.

Although African Folktales are forms of oral traditions among Africans and a reflection of African people, it faces some challenges being accepted by the other continents. One of the challenges is the language barrier. Most of the African Folktales are written, sung, or said in African Languages which is foreign to the other parts of the world. Some of these African languages do not have their meaning or adequate interpretation or equivalent translation in other languages. As such the translation of an African work written in one of the African Languages can give a different meaning to it and then lose its value.

A classic example is the first novel to be written in the Yoruba Language[19], Ogboju Ode Ninu Igbo Irunmale[20] by D.O. Fagunwa which was first published in Nigeria in 1939. The novel is about

Akara-Ogun, son of a brave warrior and a wicked witch-as he journeys into the forest, encountering and dealing with unforeseen human forces, engaging in diverse spiritual and moral relationships that determine his fate. It is a successful depiction of the mythic imagination; the narrative unfolds a terrain where, just as in Yoruba cosmology, human, natural and supernatural, beings are compellingly and wonderfully alive at once. The novel also explores the difference between the Christian beliefs of Africa's colonizers and the continents traditional religions[21].

Fagunwa in his work used a lot of complex Yoruba words and deep proverbs which have little or no equivalent translation in English. So for one to translate Fagunwa's work, such a person must be exceptionally sound in English. Prof Wole Soyinka stood up to that challenge.

The Nobel Prize-winning author Wole Soyinka translated D.O. Fagunwa's work in 'Forest of a Thousand Daemons' while imprisoned during the Nigerian Civil War in the 1960s. Although Wole Soyinka did a wonderful job translating the novel, he faced some criticism. One of the major criticisms was that he coined non-existent English words to fit some Yoruba interpretation which did not do justice to the meanings.

Another Challenge is the unrealistic nature of some folktales. Although Critics have criticized how folktales are filled up with myths, unrealistic exaggeration, a handful of impracticability, and devoid of authenticity, the purpose of folktales is to mirror reality. Folktales use literary tools like metaphors, paradoxes, oxymoron, and so on to convey its message. Conclusively, the main purpose of African folktale is primarily to teach moral lessons at the end of the story.

Conclusion

This article has looked at African philosophy, the impact of proverbs and folktales on African Culture and its challenges. It is worthy of note that even in this changing times, African creative writer who wants to stay relevant must not abandon their Culture and tradition which distinguishes them from other creative writers from other parts of the world. The achievement of an African writer should not only be to tell African stories but to seek to illuminate the African culture which is slowly fading away in contemporary Africa. It is hoped that African folktales and proverbs will motivate young readers and other readers around the world with a high sense of curiosity to research more on African Oral literature and tradition and dispel the idea that Africans are illiterates.

References

Bello S, Culture and Decision Making in Nigeria, Lagos: National Council for Arts and Culture, 1991.

Chinyere Ojiakor (Ph.D) And Nkechi Ezenwadu, "The Influence Of African Folktale In Wole Soyinka's Forest Of A Thousand Daemons And Amos Tutuola's The Palm-Wine Drinkard", Global Journal of Applied, Management and Social Sciences (GOJAMSS); Vol.14, September 2017; P.226 – 237 (ISSN: 2276 – 9013)

Elmarie Costandius, 'An Exploration Of The Use Of African Proverbs And Metaphors in A Visual Communication Design Course, Research Paper, Faculty of Education', University of the Western Cape, May, 2007, /https://core.ac.uk/display/58913254? utm_source=pdf&utm_medium=banner&utm_campaign=pdf-decoration-v1/

Gabriel E. Idang, African Culture and Values', Department of Philosophy, University of Uyo, Uyo, Akwa Ibom State, Nigeria, Volume 16 No 2, Print ISSN 1561-4018, 2015

Gyekye, Kwame, "African Ethics", The Stanford Encyclopedia of Philosophy (Fall 2011 Edition), Edward N. Zalta (ed.), URL = <https://plato.stanford.edu/archives/fall2011/entries/african-ethics/>.

John C. Ekei, "The Impact Of Philosophy In The Interpretation Of African Values With Particular Reference To Igbo Cultural values"

Jones M. Jaja, 'Myths in African concept of reality', Vol 6(2), International Journal of Educational Administration and Policy Studies, ISSN 2141-6656, 2014

Kanu Ikechukwu Anthony, 'The Meaning and Nature of African Philosophy in a Globalising World' Volume 1, Issue 7, ISSN 2349-0373 (Print), International Journal of Humanities Social Sciences and Education (IJHSSE) 2014

Ki-Zerbo, General history of Africa. London: Heinemann. (1981).

Kuzwayo, E.K.. African wisdom. Cape Town: Kwela. 1998

Merriam Webster Dictionary<https://www.merriam-webster.com/dictionary/folktale>

McKenna, J.F. The proverb in humanistic studies: Language, literature and culture – theory and classroom practice. The French Review, 48(2), December, 1974.

Ngozi Onmoha Orji, 'Proverbs and their Cultural Significance', 2013, www.AfroStyleMag.com

Endnotes

[1] Ki-Zerbo General history of Africa. London: Heinemann. (1981).

[2] Jones M. Jaja, 'Myths in African concept of reality', Vol 6(2), International Journal of Educational Administration and Policy Studies, ISSN 2141-6656, 2014

[3] Gyekye, Kwame, "African Ethics", The Stanford Encyclopedia of Philosophy (Fall 2011 Edition), Edward N. Zalta (ed.), URL = <https://plato.stanford.edu/archives/fall2011/entries/african-ethics/>.

[4] A language in Nigeria

[5] A language in Ghana

[6] Gyekye, Kwame, "African Ethics", The Stanford Encyclopedia of Philosophy (Fall 2011 Edition), Edward N. Zalta (ed.), URL = <https://plato.stanford.edu/archives/fall2011/entries/african-ethics/>.

[7] John C. Ekei, "The Impact Of Philosophy In The Interpretation Of African Values With Particular Reference To Igbo Cultural values"

[8] Gabriel E. Idang, African Culture and Values', Department of Philosophy, University of Uyo, Uyo, Akwa Ibom State, Nigeria, Volume 16 No 2, Print ISSN 1561-4018, 2015

[9] Bello, S. 1991. Culture and Decision Making in Nigeria. Lagos: National Council for Arts and Culture.

[10] Elmarie Costandius, 'An Exploration Of The Use Of African Proverbs And Metaphors in A Visual Communication Design Course, Research Paper, Faculty of Education', University of the Western Cape, May, 2007, /https://core.ac.uk/display/58913254?utm_source=pdf&utm_medium=banner&utm_campaign=pdf-decoration-v1/

[11] McKenna, J.F. The proverb in humanistic studies: Language, literature and culture – theory and classroom practice. The French Review, 48(2), December, 1974.

[12] Ngozi Onmoha Orji, 'Proverbs and their Cultural Significance', 2013, www.AfroStyleMag.com

[13] Ngozi Onmoha Orji, 'Proverbs and their Cultural Significance', 2013, www.AfroStyleMag.com

[14] It is a Bantu-speaking ethnic group in South Africa.

[15] Kuzwayo, E.K.. African wisdom. Cape Town: Kwela. 1998

[16] Chinyere Ojiakor (Ph.D) And Nkechi Ezenwadu, The Influence Of African Folktale In Wole Soyinka's Forest Of A Thousand Daemons And Amos Tutuola's The Palm-Wine Drinkard, Global Journal of Applied, Management and Social Sciences (GOJAMSS); Vol.14, September 2017; P.226 – 237 (ISSN: 2276 – 9013)

[17] Merriam Webster Dictionary<https://www.merriam-webster.com/dictionary/folktale>

[18] Chinyere Ojiakor (Ph.D) And Nkechi Ezenwadu, The Influence Of African Folktale In Wole 's Forest Of A Thousand Daemons And Amos Tutuola's The Palm Wine Drinkard, Global Journal of Applied, Management and Social Sciences (GOJAMSS); Vol.14, September 2017; P.226 – 237 (ISSN: 2276 – 9013)

[19] A Language in Nigeria (West Africa)

[20] Forest of a Thousand Daemons

[21] Chinyere Ojiakor (Ph.D) And Nkechi Ezenwadu, The Influence Of African Folktale In Wole 's Forest Of A Thousand Daemons And Amos Tutuola's The Palm Wine Drinkard, Global Journal of Applied, Management and Social Sciences (GOJAMSS); Vol.14, September 2017; P.226 – 237 (ISSN: 2276 – 9013)

MYTHOLOGY

HEAVEN WAS A PLACE ON EARTH: HOW ANCIENT CELTIC MYTHOLOGY OF THE OTHERWORLD SHAPED MODERN WORLDVIEWS

BY MEGAN MCCAFFREY

The high king, Bran, was taking a walk in the forest. While walking, he heard some mysterious music. He followed the sound, until he grew tired and fell asleep. When he awoke, he found a silver apple branch and a beautiful woman singing of an isle of women. With this song in his heart and the silver branch in hand as proof of invitation, he built a ship and sailed across the sea with a few of his men. He and his men lived happily in this otherworldly place for what they guessed was an earthly year or two until homesickness set in. They were warned by the queen of this fantasy place not to return to Ireland, but could not resist. They set sail. As they neared Ireland's coast, they realized more than just a year or two had passed. The rugged, craggy coast had been reshaped over hundreds of years. This was not the Ireland they had longed for. Ignoring this, the most homesick of the men jumped ship and swam to the coast crying tears of joy, but as soon as he reached his home, he turned to dust. He had vanished before his crewmates' eyes.

Ireland was no longer their home. They could no longer set foot there. They had to turn around and go back to the Isle of Women. Or perhaps they returned nowhere, doomed to wander the high seas, because they were no longer of this world.

This ancient Celtic mythology has shaped religions, nations of people, metaphysics, and maybe even our current worldview.

Celtic Otherworld

As most mythologies or religions with a belief in the afterlife would suggest, the world of the dead exists above, below or perhaps both. But for the ancient Celts, it existed alongside the land of the living, just barely outside the day-to-day functions of its inhabitants, separated only by a veil that could thicken and thin based on times, events, the weather or its location. This veil could thin enough that a living being could walk right into that land of immortality as if crossing a bridge. This concept was known instead as the Otherworld.

The Greeks had Hades, the Underworld where you must cross the River Styx to access, and Mount Olympus, way high atop the highest mountain in the land. The Egyptians had Duat and of course, Christianity has Heaven and Hell. The Norse had Valhalla, a great hall for those that have died in battle and for the rest, Folkvang, a field, and though it may be unclear if they were located above or below, the traveler had to be dead to get there.

This Otherworld was the home of Celtic gods and fairies. It served as a respite between lives or visits to the land of the living. By most accounts, this Otherworld or these otherworldly places, were beautiful, peaceful places of rest and plenty. It was a place where mortals could get a taste of immortality. But to paraphrase Hamlet's soliloquy, it was from whose borne no traveler returned. When people went missing, it was often assumed that they had crossed over into the Otherworld. A fairy had spirited them away. [elaborate]Time in Otherworld ran differently. An hour could be a day and a year could be decades or even centuries. Could one even survive the shock of going from one world to the next? Could the glitch in the matrix be too much for the mortals? [move one of the legends here?]

The great poet, Oisin, was also lured to the Otherworld by a beautiful, golden haired woman that he married when he realized he could not return. His wife, Niam, the daughter of an Otherworld king, grew tired of his whining and decided she would allow him to go back to his home, Ireland, for one day. The conditions of this arrangement were that he had to stay atop a magical steed she loaned him, and if his feet touched the ground, he would be ruined.

Homesick, he agreed. He was obeying his wife-boss until some boys sassed him. In response, he tried to move a boulder on horseback. He succeeded in moving the stone, but lost his balance and for a brief second, his foot touched his home soil. He immediately withered until he turned to dust and floated off in the breeze.

For the Celts, looking at the Otherworld as a place that could be stumbled upon, and from where one could not return undoubtedly shaped their worldview and gave us such enduring mythology as: Samhain traditions, headless horsemen, banshees, and fairies. This also shaped the concept of "thin places", those places where Heaven and Earth sit closer together, where even mere mortals can communicate with the divine. Could it even have introduced us to concepts of physics? [metaphysics instead?]

Thin Places

Depending on the tradition (Welsh or Irish) or the time period, the Otherworld could be everywhere or nowhere at the same time. They could be westward islands or they could be just beyond, just waiting for an occurrence to thin them and make them visible. These places were just beyond reach—either beckoning or recoiling from its searcher— one could only get there via a mystical, divinely-led quest or by invitation, as if a mythical Sandals resort but with a harsher check-out policy.

These thin places where one could travel between worlds occurred at times of transition, such as spring (especially on or around Beltane, May 1) and autumn (especially on or around Samhain, November 1), twilight and midnight. They occurred on sacred sites such as mounds and graves. They occurred where land, water and air met: i.e. caves, where air meets land, mists and fogs, where air and water meet, and in particular, places where water and land meet such as bogs, river beds, seashores, and especially islands.

Thin places were both revered and feared and must have cultivated metaphysical understanding of the world around the Celts. Nothing was always what it seemed. Mortals and immortals could tumble around each other in the time and space continuum. The worlds were vast and yet small.

It must have seemed no less than fantastical to live in such a world where the ordinary and the divine touched. Yet the uncertainty of it had to be respected. Only legends could give clues as to what lie on the other side. One must be careful and knowledgeable of their surroundings at all times or be lured away, tricked, treated, or gone forever to an unknown land.

Samhain and the Church

Early Christians were certain of an afterlife but no one could be certain of exactly how that afterlife was organized. It seems plausible that they could have entertained the notion of multiple planes of existence for the deceased. It could also explain these otherworldly creatures that the Celts were unwilling to forget.

The Church was having marked trouble infiltrating the notoriously proud (or stubborn) and superstitious Celts. A decree from Pope Gregory the First gave Christian missionaries the permission to incorporate pagan celebratory traditions into early church teachings as long as they diminished or eradicated the local populace's belief and reliance of their former deities. Therefore, the feast day of sacred Samhain became All Saints day and All Souls Day, previously dubbed All Hallows', which evolved into the modern-day Halloween or El Día de los Muertos customs we practice today.

Seeing as how the Otherworld was so close, and gods, fairies or their beasts could come and go unfetteredly on Samhain and the days preceding, the Celts took to disguising their children to confuse the various and sundry Otherworld creatures so that their offspring would not be abducted. Out of respect for the dead, the living would go to homes and offer a song for a dead loved one in exchange for cakes. Feasts were prepared and some of the food was left out for the dead or to ward off malicious spirits that may have been thinking of doing harm to that house or its residents.

I am also inclined to believe that this belief in the Otherworld could have been the predecessor to the Christian belief of Limbo. Certain souls were believed to not be able to enter Heaven nor Hell due to their transgressions on Earth. Chief of these were victims of suicide. As a result, these poor souls were doomed to wander somewhere between living and dead for all eternity. Were these the souls that were tormented or did they torment? And what if those creatures they met on the other side were fickle?

Mythical Creatures

One of the most enduring Celtic mythological creatures in modern vernacular is the fae folk, the good people, the gentry, or, to the lay person, fairies. Like people and the gods, these fairies could be good or evil, or just bored and creating mischief. They roamed about freely whenever the veils between worlds thinned leaving destruction in their wake. The tales of fae mischief are legendary and included, but are not limited to: tricking people into getting lost, switching healthy babies for sick ones, and abductions. The latter reasons caused people to live in fear and devolve into superstitions to protect themselves.

The most fearsome of these fairies was the banshee. The banshee is styled as a wailing woman in white and her cries are said to signal death or doom. She herself has even been depicted as taking away children into the Otherworld.

It could be commonalities in folklore, but the banshee figure strikes me as being eerily similar to La Llorona of Latino lore. La Llorona, the weeping woman, is a woman in a wet, white gown. The tales differ a little based on region, but it is most widely believed that she committed infanticide and then drown herself as a result of the ensuing guilt. She wanders around weeping for her dead children, often in areas of dangerous water. I personally do not feel this is a coincidence as the same Church cultivated religion in both areas of the world, and borrowed traditions from indigenous peoples in the process.

Another Celtic harbinger of doom was the headless horseman. Accounts differ on the exact origins of this gruesome figure, but the Celtic fertility god was closely associated with decapitation as a sacrificial rite. Dressed in black, astride a horse carrying its head in its hand, it terrorized the Irish countryside as well as other regions where the Celts resided. A Cornish-American author, Washington Irving, wrote one of the most famous and terrifying depictions of this mythology in his book, The Legend of Sleepy Hollow, which took place in post-Revolutionary War New York. Those unfortunate enough to see the headless horseman were likely unable to tell the tale unless it was coming for a loved one. Regardless, another soul would be lost to the endless depths of the Otherworld.

Metaphysics

The Celts loaned to us their concepts of more fluid life and afterlife. They seem to teach that time should be more loosely interpreted.

Considering how easily they could come and go and how they perceived the universe, it does not seem beyond belief that they could have imprinted upon us an idea that our world is layered. There is more to it than just what the naked eye can see. And not only that this world is layered, but that peeling back the layers can feel as satisfying as peeling the cellophane cover off a new cell phone screen, and now we just can't get enough.

The billionaire space race comes to mind, as well as time travel and multiverse theory.

It almost seems to be a fairytale when we hear of it: Billionaires playing with spaceships, learned scientists tinkering with time machines (just me?), but perhaps it is not such an absurd, or even new, concept. It isn't pyramids, democracy, or roads, but maybe the ancient Celts were smarter than we gave them credit for. Maybe their legacy was to invite us to explore this scientific curiosity with a silver branch or golden apple. To question but be open. To order our worlds with caution, wisdom, and maybe just a touch of credulity. After all, anything is possible.

Perhaps we continue to return to this folklore because we want to connect with our heritage, our homes and the lands therein. Perhaps it is because of our longing as modern humans to return to nature or simpler times as we maintain dependence on man-made machines. Perhaps it gives us a renewed desire to solve our societies' problems and master the future. I must confess, dear reader, that I have zero desire to return to a more primitive, natural way of existing, but I also prefer to write checks and I wrote the rough draft of this piece with pen and paper, so perhaps that is why I am exempt from that particular desire.

I look to folklore as a way of understanding how we as a society are willing to discuss our cultures with ease but not what plagues and scourges our culture and ourselves. We are hesitant to speak of our traumas, our struggles with grief or anxiety. We struggle to speak up that perhaps we are not okay, that we are far from it. We struggle to break the cycles we are sucked into: cycles of trauma, abuse, and poverty. Until we as a society are able to break these cycles, we will be unable to move forward.

This folklore represents a bygone era wrapped in nostalgia, but is also representative of a time when we were able to see with more clarity the world around us. We could imagine that we were all a little closer than far apart, that we were united in defending ourselves against the same foes. Maybe this folklore shows us that the past, present, and future are not so far apart after all. And that is magical.

Sources

Curran, Bob. "Osin's Return from the Otherworld." Complete Guide to Celtic Mythology, Appletree Press Ltd, 31 Dec 2000. Accessed 22 Oct 2021 http://www.irelandseye.com/irish/celtic_mythology/oisin_otherworld.shtm

Traynor, Jessica. "How tales of the headless horseman came from Celtic mythology." Irishtimes.com, The Irish Times, 23 Oct 2019, https://www.irishtimes.com/life-and-style/abroad/how-tales-of-the-headless-horseman-came-from-celtic-mythology-1.4060086

Sacred Texts. The Internet Sacred Texts Archive, www.sacred-texts.com/neu/celt/rac/rac27. Accessed 21 Oct 2021.

Santino, Jack. Halloween: The Fantasy and Folklore of All Hallows, September 1982, updated 2009, www.loc.gov/folklife/halloween-santino. Accessed 22 Oct 2021.

LITERATURE

POE'S CONCEPT OF DUALISTIC PRINCIPLE OF THE UNIVERSE "EUREKA!- I HAVE FOUND IT"

BY ANA NIKOLIC

Edgar Allan Poe belonged to the first generation of American writers that made that period the first creative era, a full flowering of the romantic impulse on American soil. Since America of that time was young country whose greatest concern was urban and technological expansion and industrial growth, these writers matured and worked in a constantly growing nation.

Politically, the time was ripe. The eighteenth century left a heritage of optimism about man's possibilities and lofty ideals of democracy asserted the value of individuals, regardless of class and education. Democracy elevated everyone to the same status and one is no longer part of traditional, old-world hierarchy. Philosophically, they reacted against materialistic educational theories for they found a Truth more a matter of intuition and imagination then a matter of logic and reason. They rejected mechanistic view of Universe and opted for a more organic view seeing the world more dynamic and living. Aesthetically, the Romantics were in a state of revolt, primarily against the restraints of formalism, seeing the poetry more progressive, lively and sociable. Economically, America had never been wealthier, but many felt a physic dislocation from the rising materialism since traditional values and conventional reality were not just enough for them.

Historical circumstances in the eighteenth century resulted in large alterations upon artistic level. Firstly, the development of science and technology, as main factors in creating a man's image of his position in the world had reached its fool sweep and brought new changes in society: Industrial Revolution in a second half of nineteenth century in England, American Declaration of Independence in 1776, Declaration about Humans' Rights in 1789 represent underlying examination of man's attitudes toward life.

One of the most crucial moments that had made an influence on creating the attitudes towards the literature of modern age was Locke's comprehension of individual. Locke had denied the existence of innate ideas and argued that a mind was a blank space (tabula rasa) on which physical experience writes. According to him, a mind assembles sensations congruently to the order of the physical world. That standpoint allowed the existence of not only one objective reality, but the possibility of existence of one's own reality of each individual. Another important standpoint is Cartesian dictum: Cogito, ergo sum as a point of a man's own evaluation.

Nineteenth century felt that the great historical and occult secrets were on the verge of revelation. Since writers attempted to respond to the new world by exploring new ways of treating time, space and experience they showed in their stories that time and individual identity could be expanded, contracted, looped or distorted. They, especially, described new worlds in moments of great social crisis and ebullitions. Ever since people riveted yearningly towards an endless celestial expanse, they were coming to conclusions that there could exist other worlds within the depths of the Universe. Many ancient writers of legends had become precursors of science-fiction genre. Some eighteen centuries ago before Neil Armstrong stepped on the Moon, Lucian of Samosata wrote satirical "True History", whose main hero shoved off into the Western Ocean, driven by desire to find out what was behind Herculean pillars. But, while most of ancient writers used utopian and futuristic settings for moral or satirical point, Poe was the first to employ them to examine purely material and scientific issues.

Having been raised in a house of rich Southern tobacco merchant, Poe had developed an attitude of real aristocratic gentleman. A Southern chivalric ideal was at the center of his view of life and art. His sense of order, feeling for music and idealization of women can all be traced to his upbringing. His lifelong effort to find a beauty and harmony in art has its roots in Poe's childhood, since the Bohemianism of his heritage and the strict prudence of his adopters were sufficient to cause an inner violence that had to erupt ultimately in some form. His outer life often became a more frantic seeking for pleasure while his inner life was an effort to transfer his discovery of aesthetic unity to the laws of being. These divergences are indeed perfectly justified and stem to a large extent from the duplicity of his personality. He had found a way into the dark recesses of human soul and had created a form in which its torments could find direct symbolic expression. Having been aware of a man's role in the world, he conceived his poetry as a mission to show us that we do not exist just for ourselves, but as a necessary, inevitable particle of the Universe.

The most significant drive for Poe's understanding of cosmos was induced by Galilei's teachings. Although Galileo Galilei had been charged in his time for heresy because he had agreed with Copernicus that the Earth moves around the Sun, he had paved a path to many men of science and philosophical thought who would confirm this theory. Despite the idea of Earth going round the Sun was contrary to Bible teachings, many felt that these permanently established teachings were incorrect, for people didn't even need technology to prove these statements invalid for they felt that the nature is not a static machine and that the laws of nature are mutable having some forces which set things in a perpetual motion.

Poe was one of the first thinkers who had intuited the modern cosmic theories without possessing scientific knowledge. His work "Eureka" is presented to those who feel rather than to those who think. But scientific assembles were not willing to give credit to Poe's intuition. As his explanation of the Universe results from his spirituality, for he believed that God created a matter from His own spirit, that is why it eludes rational explanation. Poe is said to have delivered more modern cosmological theories than any work of the Newtonian era. As romanticism created favorable soil for blossoming of scientific and literary thought, that's why many prominent philosophers, intellectuals and scientists turned to metaphysical sphere to recapture the ecstasy of discovery and explorations.

The title itself is a shout of triumph: "I have found it! I have found the answer!" The cry "Eureka" is originally the exclamation of the Syracusan engineer and mathematician Archimedes, when in his overflowing bath, he suddenly realized that the displacement of water by his body was the answer to a problem that he had been given to solve. When he had been asked to determine whether a particular crown was pure gold or gold alloyed silver, he had realized that gold and silver would displace different weights of water, Archimedes is said to have jumped up and run naked from his bath shouting: "Eureka!", "Eureka!", a Greek for "I have found it!"

"Eureka" represents Poe's description of the double motion of the universe. Thus, the physical world becomes essentially an energy, perpetual motion, permanent tension between centrifugal and centripetal forces, between Being and Nothingness, between attraction which is of the body and repulsion which is of the soul. Poe had realized that the Universe was based on the dualistic principle. His fissured mind reflects the resounding motion of the Universe. He saw in the diffusion of atoms all the frustrations that he had endured through his life. Because of his discordant mind, his soul wanted to roam free but his body longed to join with another being. He saw in the reunion with an undifferentiated body the one that would not suffer, relief of the frustrations and fears that followed him through his life.

Whenever it comes for a man to contemplate whether a world was a creation of God himself or it had been developed by a process of evolution, when a man wants to ascertain that seedling of our common genesis and a primordial particle of our birth it is a God he adduces to along with a superficial knowledge and scientific sources to create his own theory which depends on that how deep is his faith and vision.

Edgar Allan Poe certainly did not lack these attributes to create his own theory. Although many take amiss to him for being megalomaniac for considering not too difficult to undertake to solve the riddle of the Universe, he did it in the middle of his distress- after the death of his wife Virginia. It shouldn't surprise us that he underwent such a big project when he was most vulnerable as man's senses often sharpen when going through the toughest hardship in his own life.

Poe's base is laid in his discussion of the Godhead. Searching for Ideality through all his life he saw that the plots of God reflect universal perfection. In "Eureka" Poe asserts that the Universe follows a cycle- firstly a God's creation of Oneness in the primary particle after which comes a period of diffusion. The thought of God is to be understood as originating the diffusion- as proceeding with it-as regulating it- and finally, as being withdrawn from it upon its completion. Then commences the Reaction, the second part of the cycle. The Universe, having come fully into bloom, begins to contract, "rushing" in on itself until reunification. Once unified, the primary particle again explodes outward because the mind and heart of God forever recreate it. To modern cosmologists, the explosion of the Universe has become known as the Big Bang.

We can see that the Universe is comparable to an expanding and contracting heart. From this follows that our universe has spun from unity to diversity and that primary particle which comprises Oneness is considered to be the "natural" condition of the Universe and the diffusion of this particle into multiform particulars after the Big Bang, is considered to be "unnatural" condition.

As one of Poe's greatest fears was the loss of individuality, he saw the annihilation of self as the emanation from the Godhead or from Unity and he explains it in "Eureka" as following:

"The pain of the consideration that we shall lose our individual identity, ceases at once when a further reflect that the process is neither more nor less than that of the absorption, by each individual intelligence, of all other intelligences into its own. That God may be all in all, each must become God.[1]". (Harrison, XVI, 336) .

From this results that there must be some force which would compel matter to return to its primal condition. That force is a force of gravity. It is for gravity that all atoms rush together until the primary particle is completely colligated. As everything in differentiated universe has its counterpart, such is the case with gravity. It is the force of electricity. In the original Oneness there could have been no electricity because electricity is noticeable only when two or more differing particles are brought into proximity. Though the original particle contained no differing particles, when cosmos irradiates from that primordial Unity it depends upon repulsive impulses of electricity. Now we can conclude that one thing always stipulates for another thing. This confirms his primary axiom which renders: "In the original Unity of the First Thing lies the Secondary cause of All Things, with the germ of their Inevitable Annihilation.[2]"

In this essay Poe reminds us "of our source and of our destiny, among the myriad galaxies; of the bondage of our individual wills to the universal design; and of our physic and physical predisposition to the unifying forces of that design.[3]"

Poe concludes that ours is only one Universe of the Many, coexisting as one bubble in the cosmic froth.

Endnotes

[1] G.R. Thompson, The Selected Writing of Edgar Allan Poe, New York, London, 2004.

[2] David Grantz: http:// www.poedecoder.com/essays/eureka, p 3

[3] Ibid, p.16

EVERYMAN'S CAPITAL SINS

BY ROCIO DIKUN

St. Thomas stated: "A capital vice is that which has an exceedingly desirable end so that in his desire for it, a man goes on to the commission of many sins, all of which are said to originate in that vice as their chief source." When committed exceedingly, capital sins are said to lead to the spiritual corruption of individuals, whose lives become cluttered by vices.

The relationship the main character possesses with women is highly conflictive and, consequently, the members of the opposite sex are considered to be victims of his lust and gluttony. The first entails having an intense desire or need, generally sexual: "But I tell you that anyone who looks at a woman lustfully has already committed adultery with her in his heart" (Matthew 5:28). All through the novel, Everyman's thoughts regarding women concern mostly their sexual function in his life; he sees them as objects of his possession, and desires to be their owner at all times.

He marries young and has two children, Randy and Lonny. However, his first marriage results unsuccessful due to his unfaithfulness with a woman called Phoebe; who later on would become his second spouse and mother of his third child, Nancy. When he is around fifty years old he starts noticing women everywhere.

In Grenada, on a photoshoot for an advertisement, he meets a twenty four year old, Danish model called Merete and they embark on an intense affair. After a long time of seeing his mistress, he decides to go on trip to Paris with her; reason why he misses his mother's death. On both occasions, Phoebe makes sure he knows she is aware of the romance and finds it exceedingly humiliating. Everyman intends to lie, but she states the fact that she cannot trust him to be truthful again and refuses to forgive him. In order to redeem himself, particularly in his daughter's eyes, he marries Merete, an individual who cannot fulfil any of his requirements out of the sexual plane.

In addition, he gets sexually involved with his private nurse, Maureen, who has previously had affairs with several patients. In the novel, lust is directly connected to gluttony, described as an inordinate desire to consume more than that which one requires: "for drunkards and gluttons become poor, and drowsiness clothes them in rags" (Proverbs 23:21). It is not enough for Everyman to have a home, a loving wife and children; he always needs more; which leads to him cheating on his first wife and afterwards, on Phoebe.

Everyman's first wife is not deeply described all through the story; however, it is evident that his second spouse is a strong woman who loves him, takes care of him and supports him whenever he needs. As a matter of fact, guilty as he is, he is also aware of the great woman Phoebe is. On one occasion, after one of his several surgeries, he even manifests that he cannot imagine what his recovery would have been without her and he is determined to keep her in his life. Undoubtedly, were it not for all that happened, Phoebe is the person he could have remained his whole life with. She was the potential love of his life and wishes he had not behaved in a manner that damaged their relationship irreparably.

The third sin is envy, which embodies a painful or resentful awareness of an advantage enjoyed by another, joined with a desire to possess the same advantage: "Therefore, rid yourselves of all malice and all deceit, hypocrisy, envy, and slander of every kind. Like newborn babies, crave pure spiritual milk, so that by it you may grow up in your salvation" (1 Peter 2:1-2). Everyman's relationship with his brother, Howie, has remained good all his life; and despite the fact that Howie has been one of his most loyal supporters through his illnesses, he envies him deeply. While his brother has to go through an enormous amount of surgeries and ailments during his whole life, Howie has always enjoyed of an incredible health. As time goes by, his envy increases, and gets to its peak when he blames his brother for his poverty of health, even though he knows it is absurd.

This feeling gets the better of him and makes him commit another capital sin: wrath. Wrath is manifested in the individual who spurns love and opts instead for fury: "A gentle answer turns away wrath, but a harsh word stirs up anger" (Proverbs 15:1) Everyman loves his brother deeply but he cannot avoid feeling angry at the fact that he, being older, is healthier than him; he thinks Howie has everything he has always wanted for himself. Formerly, the brothers had been close and would always call each other a few times a month to talk and exchange moments of nostalgia from when they were kids. Nevertheless, Everyman's envy and wrath prompts him to become less forthcoming with Howie, until he practically cuts him off from his life without telling him why.

In contrast, nearly at the end of the story, Everyman thinks of Howie and believes he has lost him in the same way he has lost Phoebe and harmed his children's peace, through his own actions. He begins to feel regret and hopelessness at his "pointless, self-harming behaviour", described this way due to the fact that, by doing that, he caused his own feeling of loneliness.

When it comes to pride, a proud individual denotes excessive belief in one's own abilities, which interferes with the individual's recognition of the grace of God: "Pride goes before destruction, a haughty spirit before a fall" (Proverbs 16:18). Everyman does not remain in touch with his sons, Randy and Lonny. He has never attempted to explain what occurred with their mother. Instead of thinking in the wellbeing of his kids, he keeps his pride and claims that he could never take accountability for his actions because they would not understand.

In addition, he prefers not to talk to them at all in order to "avoid conflict." He does not even consider that he could have done something better as a father, other than to stay married to their mother. He believes himself to have made no mistakes and to have acted as he had to. From his point of view, it is inexplicable that Randy and Lonny make no attempt to understand his perspective, rather than depicting him as the worst version of himself.

Aside from being proud referring to matters regarding his sons, he is disdainful with them and their mindsets; he views their opinions as "childish, black and white terms rather than greys of a typical life." He is aware of the suffering that he has caused them, yet he chooses to continue feeding that grief. He believes that, at seventy-one, his life is fixed, and this failed relationship is irreparably broken. Neither does he take into account, nor does he care about the feelings of others; he only says and does what he desires when and how he desires.

A similar episode occurs when Nancy establishes that she had long hoped he and her mother would be together again, and all he does is tell her to accept reality as it is. He considers his life would be different and less lonely if several situations had turned out differently but he is not held responsible for the whole amount of his actions.

The sixth sin is sloth, which means to be disinclined to activity or exertion, not energetic or vigorous: "The way of the sluggard is blocked with thorns, but the path of the upright is a highway" (Proverbs 15:19). Sloth is present in many ways throughout the novel; however, in every case, it reflects the idea of choosing the easy path rather than working hard to get what he wanted or would improve his quality of life. Firstly, instead of pursuing painting as career, as he had always wanted, he lives according to his parents' wishes by getting married, having children and finding a safe advertising job.

Secondly, when his first marriage gets complicated, he seeks a solution by having an affair with Phoebe. He does not attempt to fix his relationship with his wife; he just wants to be out of it as soon as possible. Finally, all through the story, he reminds himself of the promise he had made when he was younger. Said promise involved not worrying about death until he was seventy five; as it is easier for him to pretend that nothing is happening and deny the fact that the idea of death haunts him at all times.

The seventh and last sin is greed. This vice displays the desire for material wealth or gain while ignoring the realm of the spiritual: "Having lost all sensitivity, they have given themselves over to sensuality so as to indulge in every kind of impurity, with a continual lust for more" (Ephesians 4:19). Everyman's father was the owner of an extremely successful jewellery, reason why Everyman spent most of his childhood there. He was surrounded by diamonds, a physical depiction of wealth. For his father, diamonds are "an indestructible portion of the earth though the wearer of the diamond themselves will die one day," quotation that implies that diamonds will long outlast human beings; nevertheless, owning them leads his owner, metaphorically, to acquire a portion of said immortality.

In addition, this situation relates to Everyman's greedy desire to live forever. Evidently, the idea of money has been prevalent in the protagonist's life since a very young age. His father had told his sons that it was important for working people to own diamonds, as they provided status, beauty, and never perished. Furthermore, while in Paris with Merete, he buys her an expensive diamond necklace worth more than all the stock in his father's jewellery store. By doing so, he feels a highborn person and lover. He expects to buy love and concern for him. As a matter of fact, that is precisely the reason why he did not argue against his parents' idea of pursing a well-paid traditional job.

To conclude, Everyman, consciously or not, commits the whole seven capital sins. Lust, by desiring numerous women and gluttony by not having enough with a loving wife that he feels the need to be unfaithful; pride, by not considering the wellbeing of his sons and only worry about himself; envy, for not having his brother's health which leads to him committing wrath; sloth, for consistently choosing the easy path instead of working hard and greed by desiring and acting as if having money and material goods were the mere reason for living. His actions are morally and ethically doubtful in regards to various aspects of his life and he hurt plenty of people who used to be close to him and loved him. However, even at the end of his life, all his loved ones are present in the cemetery to say farewell.

FRANKENSTEIN

BY PARKER SMITH

"How dangerous is the acquirement of knowledge and how much happier that man is who believes his native town to be the world, than he who aspires to be greater than his nature will allow."

-Mary Wollstonecraft Shelly

During this time of year, everyone likes to think of monsters whether they are vampires, werewolves, ghosts, or demons. However, there is one monster that stands as an iconic monster along with these creatures and that is Frankenstein's monster. While other creatures like vampires and werewolves have centuries worth of mythology and folklore, Frankenstein's monster came from a book written over two hundred years ago (Overly Sarcastic Production, 2017). In the year 1818, Mary Wollstonecraft Shelly wrote this classic horror story in her late teens. Shelly was inspired to create a chilling horror story when she went on vacation to Lake Geneva with her husband, Percy. Mary and Percy went to visit the house of Lord Byron and Byron challenged his guests to create the scariest story. Mary accepted the challenge and began her craft with the story of Frankenstein (TED-ED, 2017). The story seems to have carried on in various forms such as films but lost some aspects of the original text along the way.

The story also goes by another name: The Modern Prometheus. According to Greek mythology, Prometheus was a Titan who provided the gift of fire to humanity. After Zeus, the king of the gods, discovered this, he sentenced Prometheus to be bound and eaten by vultures for all eternity. So how is this story considered 'The Modern Prometheus"? Further in mythology, the fire stolen by Prometheus gave humanity knowledge and power beyond humans' potential (TED-ED, 2017). Victor provided a similar form of knowledge. Unfortunately, for Victor, the knowledge he sought is best left undiscovered.

According to the story of "Frankenstein", the monster is very different from the monster we see in movies and pop culture. Traditionally, Frankenstein is a giant and green brute with bolts on its neck. However, that is not the story at all. Frankenstein is not the monster but the man who created it, Victor Frankenstein (TED-ED, 2017). Victor was obsessed with knowledge and wanted to know everything that he possibly could. This obsession resulted in creating an abomination.

Another concept of Dr. Frankenstein is that he was not an actual doctor (Overly Sarcastic Production, 2019). In fact, he created the monster while he was in college and dropped out shortly after. Victor indulged his thirst for knowledge which made him excel in his college classes. However, his thirst was never quenched. Victor thought he could put his knowledge to good use by instilling life. This very act would become his downfall.

How Victor created the monster is not known. According to pop culture, Frankenstein infused the monster with lightning and electricity brought him to life. That is never portrayed in the text (Overly Sarcastic Production, 2017). While the process of creation is unknown, the story does display Victor's fascination with electricity after lightning struck a tree near his childhood home (Shelly, 2011,). This could lead readers to make their own assumptions, such as lightning instilling life in the monster.

When Victor first raises his creature, he is anything but proud. In fact, he was terrified. Victor ran away rejecting and abandoning the monster (TED-ED, 2017). As a result, the monster was left to fend for itself while Victor did everything in power to cover up and forget his "failing" experiment. The creature is tossed into a world he knows little to nothing about because he is about as sentient as a newborn child. With the mentality of a child, the monster is exposed to the cruelty of humanity. He was chased out of a house that he was staying in and got shot (Overly Sarcastic Production, 2017). The best way for him to retaliate was to channel his frustration and anger towards his creator, Victor Frankenstein. So the monster takes his newfound intelligence to go after him and his family and frame Victor in the process.

As for the monster itself, the creature is often seen as unintelligent and merely groans in pop culture. That is also not the case according to the text. The monster appears to be intelligent and, later on in the text, well spoken (Overly Sarcastic Production, 2017). According to the text, the monster learns how to make fire and learns how to read and speak after observing a family in a village (Overly Sarcastic Production, 2017). The monster has proven to be more sentient than is truly credited. Surprisingly, this makes the monster and Frankenstein share similar personality traits. Both characters are intelligent but while Victor is motivated to learn as much as he can, the creature is driven by vengeance and loneliness.

Frankenstein's attempt to create life is often depicted as a crime against humanity. This is because Mary Shelly was a Romantic and often appreciated nature. Frankenstein can be interpreted as a cautionary tale of taking knowledge too far or using knowledge to defy nature (Overly Sarcastic Production, 2017). Shelly was very cautious and wary towards science. She saw science as a means to explore radical ideas, which made her see the potential danger in science (TED-ED, 2017). While most creatures have supernatural origins, Frankenstein's monster was created in a science lab from a man's attempt to conquer life and death.

While the story does exhibit how knowledge can be taken too far, it is also a tale of not taking responsibility for actions. After Victor creates the monster, he does everything he can to forget his experiment and ensure that no one discovers his horrible secret. For example, the monster kills Victor's brother to retaliate against Victor. His family's housemaid is the prime suspect. Victor knows who the true killer is, but, instead of telling the truth, he keeps quiet and allows the housemaid to die for a crime she did not commit in order to protect himself. The monster then kills Victor's wife, Elizabeth, after Victor broke his promise to the monster to create a woman monster for him (Overly Sarcastic Production, 2017). This motivates Victor to chase the monster all the way to the Arctic where he meets his demise. Many lives could have been spared if Victor answered to his crime against nature.

housemaid to die for a crime she did not commit in order to protect himself. The monster then kills Victor's wife, Elizabeth, after Victor broke his promise to the monster to create a woman monster for him (Overly Sarcastic Production, 2017). This motivates Victor to chase the monster all the way to the Arctic where he meets his demise. Many lives could have been spared if Victor answered to his crime against nature.

References

Overly Sarcastic Production. (2017, October 31). Halloween Special: Frankenstein. youtube.com. Retrieved October 24, 2021, from

https://www.youtube.com/watch?v=gW0aqDUmTQA&list=LL&index=8

Overly Sarcastic Production. (2019, October 31). Halloween Special: Doctor Jekyll and Mister Hyde. youtube.com. Retrieved October 24, 2021, from

https://www.youtube.com/watch?v=3kUElZGMXm8&list=LL&index=5

Shelly, M. W. (2011). Frankenstein (kindle ed.). Amazon. unknown

TED-ED. (2017, February 23). Everything you need to know to read "Frankenstein" - Iseult Gillespie. youtube.com. Retrieved October 24, 2021, from

https://www.youtube.com/watchv=PDgu25Dsv34&list=PLJicmE8fK0Egm1AhWPoWY3qs2VgIfElOK&index=14

ART HISTORY

WOMEN'S SUFFERING AND RAGE THROUGH ART

BY AASHNA NAGPAL

Ovid's Metamorphoses includes the disturbing yet powerful story of Philomela. She is raped by her sister's husband Tereus in the forest and has her tongue cut off by him so that she does not reveal the crime to anyone. Resisting Tereus' censorship of her, she weaves a tapestry that depicts the ways in which Tereus violated her. Bringing the tapestry to her sister Procne, who is also Tereus' wife, she proclaims her truth and exposes Tereus' reality. Weaving is predominantly stereotyped as a woman's activity and Philomela uses the act of weaving to liberate herself from the oppressive silence forced upon her. The use of art to express the suffering endured and the rage experienced by women is an effective way to channelise what it means to be a woman into art.

Philomela & her Tapestry, Sir Edward Burne-Jones, 1864

Traditional art historiography is saturated with male artists. There are depictions of women, their bodies, but through the male gaze of the artists. Linda Nochlin's revolutionary essay "Why Have There Been No Great Women Artists?" in 1971 put forward essential points about the systematic hinderances that prevent women from being in the field of Arts and if they somehow make their way in, they are excluded from the records. Art historians, since the 1970s, have been working on recovering the lost works of women artists and reinstating the significance of such works.

One of the most famous women artists is undoubtedly Frida Kahlo. However, she has been conveniently appropriated by the mainstream culture for her unibrow and her attire without carrying along her ideology. With her aesthetically pleasing paintings significantly more famous, it is important to recall paintings of her that convey her suffering most evocatively. The first is a painting titled 'The Broken Column' that signifies chronic pain and isolation that Kahlo was subjected to owing to a near-death accident she suffered. The nails, the sheet and the column can be interpreted as parallels with the figure of Christ. However, the downward facing hands instead of raised hands like Christ's during his crucifixion can signify the denial of redemption for her that was available to Christ.

The second is a painting that is said to be inspired by the news report of a amurder but also a representation of Frida's pain when she found about her husband's affair with her sister. Even though the injuries in the painting are shown to be numerous and fatal, she questions how lightly a perpetrator can take the pain he inflicted, in Frida's case her husband's infidelity and terms it as 'A Few Small Nips'. The institution of marriage becomes a source of great suffering for women who are subjected to oppression, abuse and infidelity in the flawed institution.

The Broken Column, Frida Kahlo, 1944

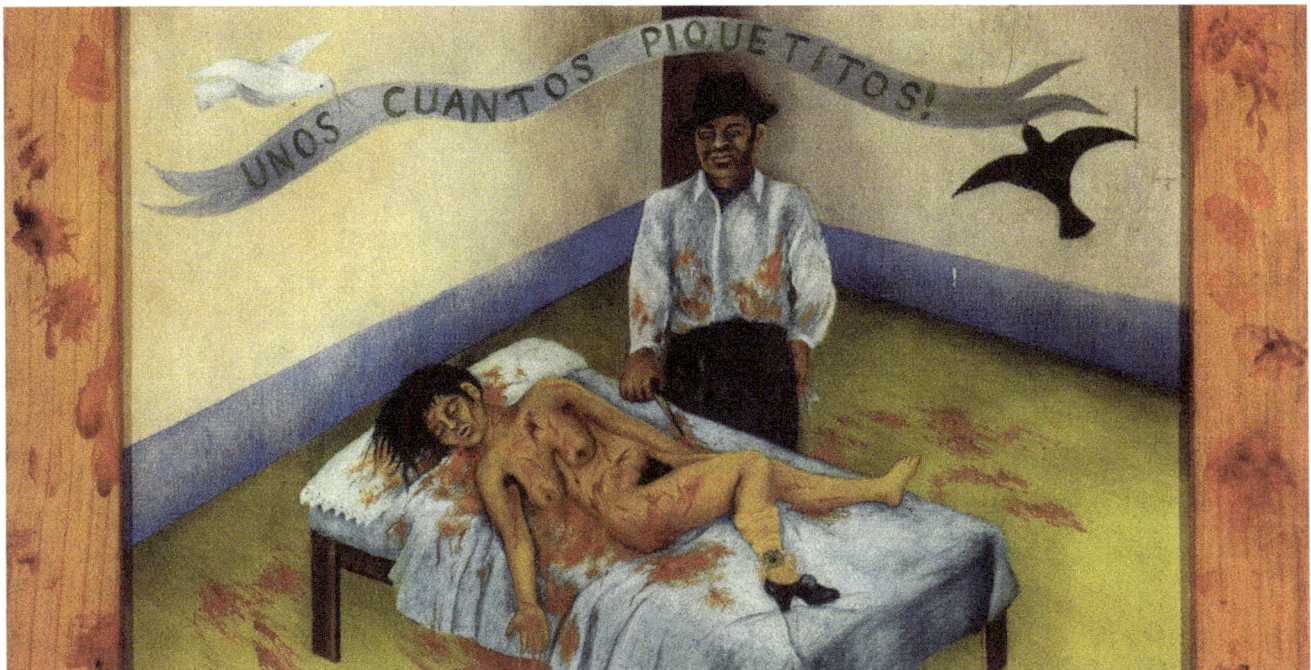

A Few Small Nips, Frida Kahlo, 1935

On the subject of the institution of marriage, a notable and gory example of women's suffering is a painting titled 'The Martyrdom of Saint Eurosia' by Giulia Lama. Lama was a Venetian painter who chartered forbidden territory in her profession by being the first woman known to draw and study the male nude from a live model (Citation) This painting shows the grotesque end a woman meets upon not following the directions of the patriarchal society. It shows the beheading of Saint Eurosia, patron saint of the city of Jaca, Spain. She was being forced into marriage with a prince and was decapitated when attempted to flee.

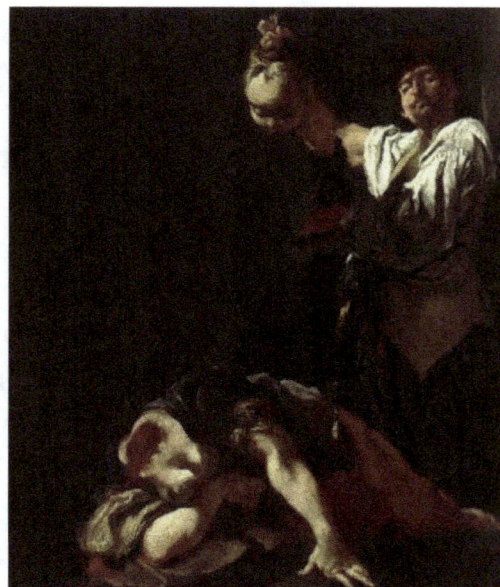

The Martyrdom of Saint Eurosia, Giulia Lama, 1728

Lama's painting is reminiscent of another painting by a Baroque woman artist Artemisia Gentileschi. Her work usually included powerful women in history and mythology. This particular painting, titled 'Judith Slaying Holofernes', although inspired by the Judith in the Bible, is said to also be a depiction of rage Gentileschi experienced herself on account of being raped by Agostino Tassi who was also a painter. (cite the article) While some critics argue to separate the sexual assault from her painting, the presence of overwhelming female rage is undeniable whether we interpret the painting with or without autobiographical influence.

Judith Slaying Holofernes, Artemisia Gentileschi, c.1620

n a similar vein is a painting by another woman Baroque artist Elisabetta Sirani, a contemporary of Gentileschi, although younger. The painting is titled 'Timoclea Killing Her Rapist' and is an artistic depiction of a tale from Plutarch's work. A high ranking member of the invading forces rapes Timoclea of Thebes and he then asks where he can find monetary spoils. Timoclea leads him to the well, suggests the money is in there and when he leans in, she shoves him in the well. She keeps throwing boulders until he dies. Instead of capturing the violation, Sirani captures the moment when Timoclea takes justice in her own hands.

n a similar vein is a painting by another woman Baroque artist Elisabetta Sirani, a contemporary of Gentileschi, although younger. The painting is titled 'Timoclea Killing Her Rapist' and is an artistic depiction of a tale from Plutarch's work. A high ranking member of the invading forces rapes Timoclea of Thebes and he then asks where he can find monetary spoils. Timoclea leads him to the well, suggests the money is in there and when he leans in, she shoves him in the well. She keeps throwing boulders until he dies. Instead of capturing the violation, Sirani captures the moment when Timoclea takes justice in her own hands.

Timoclea Killing Her Rapist, Elisabetta Sirani, 1659

There is a line of thought that argues that emotions in women's art is limited to their suffering. Not only is this paradigm narrow, it dismisses the women artists' right to portray what was marginalised for centuries. In the paintings of male artists since times immemorial, women are objects on display, often nude. The patriarchal system of the society refuses to allow women the space to express natural human emotions. It is because patriarchy has made women suffer that art by women reflects deep suffering. But the exceptional women artists simultaneously transcend this suffering through art as well as depictions of female rage. Rage and anger are stereotyped as masculine emotions but artists as back as the seventeenth century were inserting female rage into the narrative. Till today, a woman who is either crying or yelling is labelled as hysterical and unstable. The exceptional women artists in this essay are just a few examples of the revolutionary artistic endeavour by women that has been in motion and problematises what it means to be a woman through a medium of art that men largely reserved for themselves for too long.

These and so many more artists continue to challenge the gatekeeping of the Western art canon by creating work that simply can not be ignored.

OTHER ARTICLES

THE ANATOMY OF A WORD: MARTYRDOM IN THE TUDOR ERA

BY MADILYN GRACE PHELPS

Tied to the stake, his last words the prayer and the anthem "None, but Christ!" as the flames engulfed him. His allegiance was to God, his devotion was to scripture and scholarship and his fate was to be brave for all who came after him.

She was barely 25, famed for her wit, beauty, and dedication to the New Faith. The first woman to petition for divorce in England based on religious differences, the first woman tortured on the Rack. The ropes could not loosen her tongue or shake her faith.

Daughter of a royal Duke and Duchess, sister to an Earl, niece of two kings, and the granddaughter of the Kingmaker. Such an illustrious background meets its end as the elderly noblewoman is hacked to death on the scaffold. Being one of the last of a dynasty and the mother of a suspected traitor should not warrant a death sentence.

The etymology of the word "martyr" dates back to pre-12th century, meaning "a person who voluntarily suffers death as the penalty of witnessing to and refusing to renounce a religion." The pious connotation with this word seems to be lost given the myriad of situations people assign themselves to as martyrs, secular or religious. Such people assume the title to themselves, passively accepting hardships and not fighting back against it, believing apathy is a sound substitute. Whereas those we think of as martyrs for such a personal cause, we think of true bravery in the face of death, experienced in an oppressive society, where dominant groups lord over minority races, religions or other oppressed groups. The key characteristic of a martyr is one who is seen as a representative of a larger group they belong to that is being discriminated against. That means that martyrdom is a title bestowed on one after death and recognized as such for years to come. The complicated theological debate around martyrdom arises from the dominant political forces at play.

Today, we have the benefit of hindsight and can easily spot someone who suffered under oppression and decided to act against it even unto death. During the reign of Henry VIII, John Lambert, Anne Askew and Margaret Pole have retroactively been given this title, for their "illegal" religion and as blameless victims, respectively. Their backgrounds, faiths, and reasons for the circumstances of their deaths all vary. Due to the tumult and capriciousness of Henry VIII's reign and beliefs, this is not surprising. In fact, many victims slain during his reign have been referred to as martyrs at one point or another. The interest in these peoples' circumstance is how they represented the shifting political alliances during the Reformation and how big a role religious supremacy played in politics.

John Lambert (Nicholson) (?-1538) began to find flaws in the practice of the Catholic faith while a fellow at Queen's College and found refuge in a theological-humanist philosophy group that met in a tavern. This mold is significant because later revolutionary groups found their origins in discussion, and debate over philosophy and religion over food and drink. Especially so because in the 16th century, religion was the guiding force in political policy and everyday existence. By the early 1530's, religious life in England was in tumult. The spread of Protestantism in mainland Europe had reached England. Protestant writers' books were published and smuggled to be read, the King had split with the Roman Catholic Church to marry an Evangelical woman, had appointed a German-born archbishop of Canterbury with Protestant leanings, and his chief minister Thomas Cromwell (Lambert's Cambridge classmate) had begun a widely disliked campaign of closing Catholic monasteries and seizing the riches inside.

This did not mean every English person was automatically Evangelical or that they would not relinquish their ties to Rome without a fight. Many Protestant writers and priests, such as William Tyndale and John Frith, came under fire from conservative bishops. Lambert, sensing the danger, tried to keep his head down and began a career as a Latin and Greek tutor. Those in charge eventually caught up with him and he was put on trial for heresy. Their evidence was his denunciation and disbelief of the religious tenet of transubstantiation, or that the body and blood of Christ was transformed into wine and bread at Mass. He did not recant, and he was sentenced to die at the stake. His former classmate Cromwell wept at his execution and Lambert would be remembered through John Foxe's Book of Martyrs. His sentence, his charge and his remembrance bear a striking resemblance to a fellow evangelical less than a decade later. Her fate would rest not solely on her actions, but on her associations and those who sought to rob her of her agency.

It would be a disservice to simply apply the label of modern woman to Anne Askew (1521-1546). This is because her actions were and unprecedented and radicals for her time, centered around her want of an independence not afforded to women specifically. Born to a gentry family in the North, she began to turn away from Catholicism in her teens when her brothers were essentially forced into the Pilgrimage of Grace, a widespread protest by Catholics in the face of the growing evangelical influence of Cromwell's tenure as minister. The first English translations of the Bible and the legal allowance of ordinary citizens to read the bible for themselves fundamentally changed Anne's life. Her Bible study was off-putting to her traditional Catholic husband (who she was forced to marry as he was promised to her sister, who died, and her father was not about to give up the dowry). Anne had already declared herself separate from the heteronormative mold by refusing to take her husband's last name and her continued religious obstinance. According to church doctrine, this meant he had to expel her from her home. That was fine with her, and she sought to legally divorce herself from her husband, citing their religious differences. Much as Henry VIII sought out theology to justify his marriage and divorce to Catherine of Aragon, Anne sought out advice from St. Paul that said it was her duty to leave an impious man. Proving centuries ahead of her time, Anne was the first woman in England to do this.

Her first concrete step to independence took place in London. First, she asked her brother, who worked for Henry VIII, to plead her case of divorce as she believed he would grant it as he did his. During this time, she took rooms in an inn and began making money selling bibles, tracts, and papers. She also began preaching and debating fellow radical Protestants, quickly becoming renowned for her charm, wordplay, beauty, and exceptional scholarship. She soon caught the attention of the Queen Catherine Parr herself, and she invited Anne to her Bible study group of noblewomen. Underneath this life of contentment, piety and networking was a seething conspiracy to undo not Anne, but Queen Catherine.

By this point, King Henry had remarried four times, three Catholics (Jane Seymour, Anne of Cleves, and Catherine Howard) and finally Catherine Parr, a noblewoman whose leanings were distinctly Protestant. her views and own published works had won her friends, but also earned her many enemies. The traditional and Catholic faction at court was still quite strong, and they sought to prove to the King that the Queen was a heretic. They planned to do that through Anne. They arrested, charged, and convicted her for heresy, for the same renunciation of transubstantiation that John Lambert had professed. They also interrogated her about her association with prominent women, hoping to use her to name names. Anne refused and they resorted to torture, an act so unprecedented and disgusting the jailor had to step out and he ran to the King to get him to stop it. The King did not, and Anne was torn limb from limb by Lord Chancellor Thomas Wriothesley and Sir Richard Rich, two noblemen who equally took unexpectedly brutal acts against such a young woman. It was so gruesome, Anne had to be carried on and sat in a chair for her to be burned, as she could not support her weight. She, and those she was burned with, refused to recant. Onlookers were so taken with shock and grief; some threw gunpowder on them so they would die quicker. She too was written by Foxe in his book, along with her own memoirs of her imprisonment, proved that this martyr would not go quietly.

Margaret Pole, Countess of Salisbury (1473-1541) was once one of the richest women in England and only one of two women in the 16th century who held a peerage title in her own right. The other was Anne Boleyn, Marquess of Pembroke. Her royal background (her father and mother were George, Duke of Clarence and Isabel Neville, Duchess of Clarence; her uncles were Kings Edward IV and Richard III), her wealth, and her relation to royalty should have guaranteed her a life of ease and luxury, piety, and traditional ways. Instead, it brought her sorrow. Her life seemed to be one tumbling sadness after another and by the end of her life, her only comfort was in her faith. She was a staunch Catholic who would not have been subject to the shifting religious alliances of the King. She was not a martyr in the sense that she was standing up for her beliefs unto penalty of death and being recognized by others. Instead, she was punished for the actions of her son Cardinal Reginald Pole, who all but declared war on Henry VIII for his Reformation and supported efforts to undermine his reign. Like Anne Askew, Margaret was punished for her proximity to what was perceived as a bigger threat to not solely the King, but England as a whole.

Orphaned at five years old, Margaret grew up with her brother Edward in her uncle and aunt's household until their deaths in 1485. At that point, her brother was seen as a threat to the Tudor monarchy. He was named as the heir to Richard III after the death of his own son and Edward was imprisoned to prevent his undertaking an uprising. That did not stop others doing it in his name and in 1499, the 24-year-old Edward was executed for treason. This must have been wrenching for Margaret. Her parents died when she was an incredibly young child and whatever grief she may have felt for her aunt and uncle had to be put to the side. Her marriage to Sir Richard Pole, while arranged to quell any chance of usurpation, appeared to have been a close one with multiple children, providing her with some happiness. Her proximity to the Plantagenet dynasty and those loyal to the House of York (or as equally plausible, simply against the Tudors), meant she could not take any action even conceivably disloyal. This personal abstention from dissent did not extend to her son Reginald.

Reginald publicly denounced the formation of the Church of England and King Henry separating England from the Roman Catholic Church. There were still many loyal Catholic factions present in England and were still loyal to Catherine of Aragon, and her daughter Mary (the future Mary I). Against popular European support, Reginald undertook a campaign to promote his beliefs and gather a large enough conglomerate to support a usurpation of Henry VIII. Margaret herself dismissed his ideas as folly and made it clear she did not support her son. Nevertheless, the King did not appreciate such dissent and after several attempts to assassinate him failed, Cromwell and he took their revenge on his family. Margaret's sons lost standing and land and were executed. She herself had her land and titles confiscated and was put on trial for treason and was convicted. The crutch of the case was a tapestry bearing the Five Wounds of Christ, symbolizing bother Catholic faith and support for her son. Considering this was found six months after the first time her home was searched, it is safe to say this was likely invented evidence meant to bolster the case against her. She was sentenced to death but was not given a death. This meant that the King could sentence his mother's cousin to death whenever he wanted.

Her time in the Tower was marked by isolation, and discomfort. The stone building was cold, with no ventilation and none of the comforts she was used to. Even with a litany of servants and fur trimmed clothing from Queen Catherine Howard, Margaret's final two years would have certainly been a solemn reflection of her tumultuous, and tragic existence. To live in the same building where her father and brother were executed was certainly not lost on the noblewoman. The day in May came without warning. Accounts differ from what happened next. What is certain is that an elderly lady charged unjustly was put to death by a king many were coming to see as mercurial at best and tyrannical at worst. Margaret scratched a poem into the walls of her cell. Its words survived to the day in 1886, when she was recognized as a martyr for the Catholic faith. She would not relinquish that faith, for fear of earning the King's ire. While it may not be the exact reason she died, it certainly fits into the denotation of a martyr. John Lambert, Anne Askew and Margaret Pole lived in one of the most politically tumultuous times of modern history, bore witness to social and religious strife and were punished for refusing to toe the line. They stood fast to their faiths, did not leave quietly, and were surely rewarded with their place in paradise.

"For traitors on the block should die;

I am no traitor, no, not I!

My faithfulness stands fast and so,

Towards the block I shall not go!

Nor make one step, as you shall see;

Christ in Thy Mercy, save Thou me!"

-Margaret Pole, Countess of Salisbury

DALMATIA – EUROPE'S FORGOTTEN COUNTRY

BY RHYS DALEY

In June 1898, an explosion rocked the Adriatic island of Krk (Veglia). Among the dead was a man in his seventies called Tuone Udaina, the last known speaker of the Dalmatian language. Udaina was a native speaker not of Dalmatian but of Venetian, which over the centuries had heavily influenced Dalmatian; it was the language of his parents and he learnt it through listening to their private conversations, and he had spoken it with his grandmother[1]. In the years before his death, he was visited by the Italian linguist Matteo Bartoli who wished to study his language. Though it had been roughly twenty years since he had spoken his Vegliot dialect of Dalmatian and his pronunciation was very rusty[2], Udaina was able to recall approximately 2,800 words, stories, folklore, songs, accounts of his life, and responses to questions about grammar[3], all of which Bartoli wrote in a book, first published in Italian and then German (Das Dalmatische)[4]. Although his native Venetian heavily tainted his recollection of Dalmatian, Bartoli was nonetheless able to preserve a profound insight into this language, but no audio recording was ever made[5].

Udaina was the last of the Dalmatians, a people whom once stretched along the coastline of Croatia, Bosnia & Herzegovina, and Montenegro, and the extensive and plentiful islands of the Adriatic. Nestled in the islands, the last, isolated vestiges of this language and its culture lived and endured. A culture and history of trade, commerce, endurance, plight, and the calling of the sea. With Udaina died the last gasps of a people, language, and civilisation once resplendent in the sun-drenched shores of the Balkans, leaving behind the cities they built and the islands upon which they dwelt for those who would notice the marks they left. But who were they? What were their ways? Why had they diminished to but one island? And why, with both a bang and a whimper, did they end?

Sons of Rome

Dalmatia is a region on the eastern shores of the Adriatic, taking its name from the ancient Dalmatae tribe of Illyrian people, whom inhabited their namesake region of Illyria in the time of the Romans. Dalmatia region became a Roman province in 9 AD after the Illyrian Wars[6], and the region steadily became Romanised. By the 4th Century, the coast of this region and the islands had been fully Romanised[7]. Beyond the coast, the cities were fully Romanised, but the hinterland very much retained its native Illyrian language, religion, and customs[8]. After the collapse of the Western Roman Empire in 476 AD, the development of Dalmatia into something

49

HERMES MAGAZINE

distinct and unique became expedited[9]. Central to this was that Dalmatia was contested; torn between factions wanting its riches and coasts. Fierce and often violent struggle and dispute would go on to define the history of this land and shape much about it. Ravaged by Goths and contested between Eastern and Western Rome[10], the governor Julius Nepo was the brief vestige of Western Rome holding out against the Gothic forces of Odoacer in Italy before Theoderic the Great conquered the region and absorbed it into his kingdom in 493[11].

Great Roman cities arose in this land, settled by Roman colonists from Italy when Roman control began[12]. The Romans made Salona their regional capital and built roads linking their cities of Aquileia, Dyrrachium (Durrës), Spalatum (Split), and others[13], which "enabled the establishment of an open, cosmopolitan urban core for the province on the coast.[14]" Salona, and also Spalatum very nearby, were chief of Adriatic splendour. The Dalmatian capital "developed into a cosmopolitan centre of the Adriatic.[15]" The birthplace of the emperor Diocletian[16], it was the site of a resplendent and intricate palace which dominated the skyline and stands still today in the Croatian city of Split. The expert Roman historian Edward Gibbon describes the antique site:

It covered an extent of ground consisting of between nine and ten English acres. The form was quadrangular, flanked with sixteen towers. Two of the sides were near 600, and the other two near 700 feet in length. The whole was constructed of a beautiful free-stone... Four streets, intersecting each other at right angles, divided the several parts of this great edifice, and the approach to the principal apartment was from a very stately entrance, which is still denominated the Golden Gate[17].

This palace – the heart of Salona – would prove a refuge for its people. Dalmatia became contested and torn again, ravaged by the Goths, Sarmatians, and Avars from the east. And as the barbarians rained the fires of war down the Dinaric mountainside to the east and scorched the sun-soaked cities of the Adriatic, the Romans of Dalmatia fled to the sea and islands such as Solta (Šolta), Brazza (Brač), Lesina (Hvar), Lissa (Vis), and Curzola (Korčula) for a haven[18], using as a fortress of safety the great palace of Diocletian," large enough for many thousands to settle. "For it was when she lay desolate, ravaged by the Avars in 639, that her homeless people, who had first fled to the islands, bethought themselves of the security offered by the strong walls of Diocletian's palace, and repaired thither and built a new town within its precincts.[19]" The final wave of destruction came with the arrival of the Slavs[20], and with it, the development of two areas of settlement; east of the Dinaric Alps, "the towns of the interior were possessed by the Slavi," and west of those craggy peaks and snowy slopes, the Romans became Dalmatians[21]. In Diocletian's palace "they lived some time in poverty, building huts of leaves and osiers and suffering much from scarcity of water, while the younger men equipped some light ships and scoured the coasts, making reprisals on their enemies so that none of the Slavs dared to go down to the sea.[22]" Further south, there was no luxury of thick walls and ramparts of stone to protect them from the Slavs, so the Romans of the cities there fled to the thin coastline and there settled the most important eastern Adriatic city in the Middle Ages (with its numbers swelled with further destruction of Salona in 449 AD) [23], crucial to the now-lost language of its people, and which would later grow into a republic of its own – Ragusa[24].

A Nation is Born

Travelling through the land in 1848, the English traveller Sir John Gardner Wilkinson describes Ragusa and its hinterland:

"The face of the country is very varied: a ridge of lofty limestone mountains separates the northern portion from Turkey, and another runs nearly parallel with the coast, close to which it approaches in the vicinity of Spalato, and extends thence to Montenegro and Albania. The highest peaks are Orien, 6,332 feet; Dinara, 6,040 feet; and Pastovo, 5,929 feet; and the largest and loftiest part of the northern range is that of Velebich, to the northeast of Zara, which measures 5,439 feet.

The inland parts of Dalmatia are diversified by undulatory ground, hills, and high mountains; many of the latter having the same rugged, barren, aspect as those of the coast… some of the islands produce pines and brushwood in great abundance, particularly Curzola… and still has the greatest quantity of wood in this part of the Adriatic.[25]"

The distinguished British architect, Sir Thomas Graham Jackson, further describes the city:

"Situated on a craggy peninsula, which was in those days insulated by a shallow marshy canal, running east and west from sea to sea on the site of the present Corse. This island, sloping gradually upward from the canal, but scarped abruptly with sheer precipices towards the sea, where the Roman refugees established themselves. [26]"

Central to the development of the city of Ragusa was the people's relations with the Slavs whom had come to dominate the lands east of the mountains, and increasingly settle coastal regions. "Opposite them, beyond the canal, on the slopes of M. Sergio, a rival colony of… Bosnians settled themselves, and across the intervening plain, the rival colonies watched one another from their respective hills… across the marshy level which afterwards became the forum of the joint community.[27]" The expansion of the city was steady and rapid. Four times, its walls were extended by the year 949, and at one point clearing Monte Sergio of oak trees and enclosing the land within new walls to grow the city; it is here that Ragusa derives its Slavic name of Dubrovnik, from Dubrava, an oak wood[28]. The two communities lived divided by a marshy channel, later filled and paved to form the Stradun, a main street that still serves significance in Dubrovnik today: *"Over the centuries the populations mixed, the channel was filled in, and the city's walls grew to encompass both parts of the settlement. But even today there's a clear distinction between the steep narrow streets leading uphill from Stradun to the north and the palaces and churches and open squares that characterise the rest of the city to the south. To their dying day, Ragusan patricians insisted they could trace their lineage back to Roman rather than Slav ancestors.[29]"*

Despite the oak which gives Ragusa its Slavic name, the Roman statesman Strabo once described the land as "sterile, unsuited to agriculture, and barely affording a subsistence to the inhabitants. [30]" Indeed, "the population of all the Ragusan territories has been estimated to be 40,000," and this "small population could not provision itself" because ""the narrow strip of coastline does not contain much arable land.[31]" As the city grew, this problem compounded, exacerbated further still by the lack of convenient routes to transport bulky grains[32]. Ragusa had to depend on its port for grain shipments, and by necessity, became a maritime power to secure their trade and maintenance of their trade networks[33]. But these trade networks would bring Ragusa into contact, contest, and conflict with a greater power to the west – a lion whose roar would be heard through the winding streets and across its islands.

On the western shore of the Adriatic lies a city with whom Ragusa would share much history, but in whose shadow it would always live: Venice. Even its inception and coming into being arose the same way. The great English historian and famous chronicler of Rome Edward Gibbon describes how "many families of Aquileia, Padua, and the adjacent towns, who fled from the sword of the Huns, found a safe, though obscure, refuge in the neighbouring islands.[34]" Whereas Ragusa had the protection of an archipelago to the west and the Dinaric Alps to the east, the Venetians turned to the protection of the bay and lagoon. "At the extremity of the Gulf, where the Adriatic feebly imitates the tides of the ocean, near a hundred small islands are separated by shallow water from the continent, and protected by the waves by several long slips of land.[35]" With both nations depending themselves upon the sea, it was only a matter of time until the Lion of St. Mark flexed its muscles against its easterly neighbour, but Venice was not the only power coveting the Ragusans.

Initially, Ragusa was under Byzantine protection for two hundred years and withstood a fifteen-month long Ottoman siege in 867-8[36]. When pirates and the Slavic polities sought dominance of the Adriatic, the Ragusans turned to their Latin cousins in Venice for alliance, and in 1001, Venice and Ragusa signed a commerce treaty[37]. Jackson argues that Ragusa's history "begins with her direct connexion with Venice and the end of her nominal dependence on the Byzantine Empire. [38]" In many ways, Jackson is right, but as much as the two city states were similar in their origins and their strength in the sea, Ragusa was much different, with a distinct Slavic twist which drove its society. Faced with Narantine (Slavic) piracy "against many Slovenian princes, as well as the free towns of Dalmatia and the Greek emperor, the Venetians gladly seized the opportunity for crushing this formidable enemy of their commerce.[39]"

One event about which Ragusan and Venetian historians vehemently disagree is the conspiracy of Damiano Giusa. Venetians claim he "tried to make himself absolute and of whom the Ragusans rid themselves by calling in the Venetians and accepting a Venetian count.[40]" Ragusan historians present a very different recollection of this event, proposing that they were already under Venetian rule and that Giusa only wanted to free Ragusa so it may rule itself[41]. According to Jackson, a third suggestion of this event is that "Damiano was a champion of the rights of the commonality then in the process of extinction by the party which was already forming itself into a compact aristocracy, and which only triumphed over him by the aid of the Venetians.

It's important to consider this historiographical divide in its context. The Venetians were the dominant maritime and trading power and outshined Ragusa in every way, and wanted to proclaim their greatness by diminishing the conquered and the subjects. The Ragusans saw themselves as still distinct and important in their own right, with their own history and their own culture, and wished to present this face to the world and did not want to be written out of their own history. Regardless of who was right, the Venetians from this point on exerted ever greater influence over Ragusa's culture and language. In his travels, Wilkinson describes how Venice clasped at the Dalmatian coast:

"The houses have much the character of Venetian buildings; and there is an air of former wealth about it, which inspires a feeling of regret for its bygone greatness. The effects of the earthquakes, visible at every turn... recall the sufferings endured by the Ragusans... Here, for the first time, the winged lion of St. Mark ceases to appear; and the absence of this emblem of Venetian subjugation, the boast of the Ragusans, cannot fail to inspire everyone with respect for a people who preserved their country from the all-absorbing power of Venice.[42]"

Venice was able to introduce much commercial reform to Ragusa. "Guilds of various trades were formed... and colonies of Ragusan traders settled in the interior of the Balkan Peninsula to open a way for commerce with Italy," and in 1216, "the island of Lagosta was bought by Ragusa from Stefano Nemagna II of Servia.43]" Its transfer to Hungarian control in 1358 allowed the city to greatly expand its fortifications[44], but the city was famously ravaged by an earthquake in

1667[45]. By this time, the Turks had been advancing across the Balkans, but their defeat at Vienna had quelled their threat, and the Venetians took advantage of their weakness by taking the city in 1699[46]. "Trade declined and the Turk, now reduced to court the favour of the Venetians whom he formerly defied, diverted the stream of his commerce towards Venice rather than Ragusa.[47]" The fall of Venice in 1797 inevitably drew the eyes of the French, Russians, and Austrians to Ragusa; when the French occupied the city in 1806, "the Republic of Ragusa ceased to exist by a word from those lips by which so many greater states than this were made and unmade. In 1814, the combined efforts of the English and Austrians drove the French from the city and from that time Ragusa followed the fate of all Dalmatia and remained under Austrian rule.[48]"

The Ragusan People

And it is under Austrian rule as the Kingdom of Dalmatia within the empire that the Dalmatian people slowly faded until that day in June 1898, with the death of Tuone Udaita, and with him the death of the last vestige of Dalmatian civilisation. Before their death, their people and culture were documented, their achievements noted, and their language (albeit briefly) recorded. "The number of Ragusan artists who worked at Florence, at Rome, and at the court of Hungary, and earned for themselves both bread and fame in foreign countries proves they had little prospect of winning either at home.[49]" Distinctive of the land they inhabited providing insufficient fertile ground for its people, sending them to the sea and depending upon lands beyond its shores, so did the people of Ragusa seek riches in other lands where they found their own barren.

Bartoli was able to transcribe thousands of words of the Vegliot dialect of Dalmatian before he died. In his work Das Dalmatische, he writes several examples:

·Pen (bread) – Latin panem

·Chesa (house) – Latin casa

Lero, Hojam, Dolerija, Jelena (names)[50]

·Nume (name) – Latin nomen

·Domnu (God) – Latin Deus

·Figl' (son) – Latin Filius

·Sore (sun) – Latin Sol

·Vint (wind) – Latin ventus

·Zia (day) – Latin deus

·Lu'a/lùja (moon) – Latin luna

·Nopte (night) – Latin nox

·Ploje (rain) – Latin pluvial

·Cad (hot) – Latin calidus

·Fgliara (iron) – Latin ferrum

·Jarba (grass) – Latin herba

Appa (water) – Latin aqua[51]

Further to these examples and more, Bartoli gives us the Lord's Prayer in Dalmatian (Latin under each line):

Ciacce nosstru, carle jesti in Cer, svetase nume attev:

Pater nosterm qi es in Coelis. Sanctificetur nomen tuum.

Neca vire Cragliestvo attevo: neca fie voglia atta.

Adveniat regnum tuum, fiat voluntas tua.

Cum jaste in Cer, assa si pre pamint. P'ra anostra

Sicut in Coelo, sic et in terra. Pamen nostrum

desvacazi da a noi astes: si prosta noi dughe

quotidianum da nobis hodie; et dimitte nobis debita

a nostre, cum sin oi prostam lu duxni anostri. Si nu

nostra, sicut et nos dimittimus debitoribus nostris. Et non

lasa noi accada in napast: nego osloboda nos de rev.

Inducas nos cadere in tentationem: sed libera nos a malo.

Owing to the different cultures and influences within Ragusa and wider Dalmatia, the matter of language wasn't simple. In a study of fifteenth-century Ragusan society, David Rheubottom describes the polyglot community of the country:

"Four languages were in everyday use. A vernacular Slavic language was likely to have been the language of the streets and domestic use. Servants and villagers began to adopt Slavic forms of their surnames... the Ragusan poet Džore Držić (1461-1501) wrote in the Slavic vernacular... Official council records make it clear that Italian was also commonly used in the city... It is known that Italian was the language of commerce and was also used in schools. Latin is a third possibility. Learned patricians would be familiar with Roman practice from their reading of the classics as well as study of the law.[53]"

Influenced by all three of the aforementioned languages, especially as Italian and increasingly Venetian became the language of patrician family life, Ragusa's native language of Dalmatian "was sufficiently important for the Senate to rule in 1472 that it should be the idiom of council discussions.[54]" Furthermore, it's important to note that Dalmatian was not a cohesive and standardised language. There existed a "variety of different dialects of Latin, affected by their social class, as well as micro- and macro-regional factors.[55]" Indeed, there were many dialects of Dalmatian from many places, including Fiume (Rijeka), Cattaro (Kotor), Jedera (Zadar), Repsa (Cres), Arba (Rab), Krk (where Udaina's Vegliot was spoken), Spalatum, and Ragusa, among which were chief, Ragusan and Velgiot (which survived the longest)[56]. Ultimately, though, because Dalmatian lost prestige to Venetian, as Ragusa was always in Venice's shadow, there wasn't enough room in the Adriadic for two maritime powers, and even though Ragusa's republic survived a little longer than Venice's, the Lion of St. Mark was the greater beast and left a greater mark.

"The continued existence of the little Republic for so many centuries is the greatest tribute to the sagacity of its rulers. Its position exposed it to constant alarms, surrounded as it was by troublesome neighbours... and the whole career of the Ragusan Republic was a struggle for self-preservation, and the maintenance of its independence in the midst of constant danger.[57]" The Dalmatians and Ragusans carved out a state out of the fires of war, and built a remarkable city hewn into the rock of the Dalmatian coastline. In a story of constant struggle, it ultimately lost out, and its very name is now merely a note in history books, overtaken by Slavic (Croatian) culture under the name of Dubrovnik. But if you take the steps of the English explorers mentioned here, if you walk the streets of Dubrovnik and notice the Venetian architecture or walk among the marvels of Diocletian's palace in Split – if you peer into history, though it wasn't preserved in their own tongues, the story of the Dalmatians is there to discover.

Endnotes

[1] Adam Ledgeway and Martin Maiden, The Oxford Guide To The Romance Languages (Oxford: Oxford University Press, 2016), p. 126.

[2] Peter B. Norton and Robert McHenry, The Encyclopedia Britannica: Macropædia - Knowledge In Depth (Chicago: Encyclopaedia Britannica, Inc., 2003), p. 623.

[3] Ledgeway (2016), p.126.

[4] Ibid.

[5] Ibid.

[6] Robert I Curtis, Garum And Salsamenta (Leiden: E.J. Brill, 1991), p. 113.

[7] Theodor Mommsen, T. Robert S Broughton and Theodor Mommsen, The Provinces Of The Roman Empire (Chicago: University of Chicago Press, 1968), p. 203-.

[8] Aleksandar Stipčević, Iliri (Zagreb: Školska knjiga Zagreb, 1974), p. 70.

[9] John B Bury, History Of The Later Roman Empire (New York: Dover, 1970), p. 405.

[10] Ibid, p. 412.

[11] Ibid, p. 426.

[12] Danijel Dzino, Illyricum In Roman Politics, 229 BC-AD 68 (Cambridge, UK: Cambridge University Press, 2010), p. 182.

[13] Ibid

[14] Ibid, p. 183.

[15] "Solin (Salona)", W3.Mrki.Info, 2021 <http://w3.mrki.info/split/solin.html> [Accessed 22 October 2021].

[16] Edward Gibbon, The Decline And Fall Of The Roman Empire (Verbatim Reprint), 1st edn (London: F. Warne and Company, 1893), p. 294.

[17] Ibid, p. 289.

[18] Sir Thomas Graham Jackson, Dalmatia: The Quarnero And Istria, 2nd edn (Oxford: Oxford University Press, 1887), p. 2.

[19] Maude M Holbach, Dalmatia, The Land Where East Meets West, By Maude M. Holbach .. (London: J. Lane, 1908), p. 71.

[20] Sir John Gardner Wilkinson, Dalmatia And Montenegro (London: Spottiswoode and Shaw, 1848), p. 274.

[21] Ibid, p. 275.

[22] Jackson (1887), p. 2.

[23] Jackson (1887), p. 287.

[24] Wilkinson (1848), p. 274.

[25] Ibid, p. 38-40.

[26] Jackson (1848), p. 288.

[27] Ibid.

[28] Wilkinson (1848), p. 277.

[29] Piers Letcher and Rudolf Abraham, Croatia (Guildford: Bradt, 2010), p. 311.

[30] Ibid, p. 40.

[31] David Rheubottom, Age, Marriage, And Politics In Fifteenth-Century Ragusa (Oxford: Oxford University Press, 2000), p. 28.

[32] Ibid.

[33] Ibid.

[34] Edward Gibbon, The Decline And Fall Of The Roman Empire, Vol. III (Boston: Phillips, Sampson, and Company, 1856), p. 447.

[35] Ibid.

[36] Jackson (1887), p. 288.

[37] Wilkinson (1848), p. 285.

[38] Jackson (1887), p. 288.

[39] Wilkinson (1848), p. 283.

[40] Jackson (1887), p. 289-90.

[41] Ibid, p. 90.

[42] Wilkinson (1848) p. 273.

[43] Jackson (1887), p. 295.

[44] Ibid.

[45] Ibid, p. 306.

[46] Ibid.

[47] Ibid, p. 309.

[48] Ibid.

[49] Ibid, p. 313.

[50] Matteo Giulio Bartoli, Das Dalmatische (Nendeln/Liechtenstein: Kraus, 1975), p. 117.

[51] Ibid, p. 224.

[52] Ibid, p. 224-5.

[53] Rheubottom (2000), p. 56.

[54] Ibid.

[55] Danijel Dzino, Becoming Slav, Becoming Croat (Leiden: Brill, 2010), p. 162.

[56] Žarko Muljačić, "O Dalmatoromanizmima U Marulićevim Djelima", Colloquia Maruliana, 12 (2003), 131-142.

[57] Jackson (1887), p. 309.

Bibliography

·"Solin (Salona)", W3.Mrki.Info, 2021 <http://w3.mrki.info/split/solin.html> [Accessed 22 October 2021]

·Bartoli, Matteo Giulio, Das Dalmatische (Nendeln/Liechtenstein: Kraus, 1975)

·Bury, John B, History Of The Later Roman Empire (New York: Dover, 1970), p. 405

·Curtis, Robert I, Garum And Salsamenta (Leiden: E.J. Brill, 1991), p. 113

·Dzino, Danijel, Becoming Slav, Becoming Croat (Leiden: Brill, 2010)

·Dzino, Danijel, Illyricum In Roman Politics, 229 BC-AD 68 (Cambridge, UK: Cambridge University Press, 2010), p. 182

·Gibbon, Edward, The Decline And Fall Of The Roman Empire (Verbatim Reprint), 1st edn (London: F. Warne and Company, 1893)

·Gibbon, Edward, The Decline And Fall Of The Roman Empire, Vol. III (Boston: Phillips, Sampson, and Company, 1856).

·Holbach, Maude M, Dalmatia, The Land Where East Meets West, By Maude M. Holbach .. (London: J. Lane, 1908), p. 71

·Jackson, Sir Thomas Graham, Dalmatia: The Quarnero And Istria, 2nd edn (Oxford: Oxford University Press, 1887).

·Ledgeway, Adam, and Martin Maiden, The Oxford Guide To The Romance Languages (Oxford: Oxford University Press, 2016), p. 126

·Letcher, Piers, and Rudolf Abraham, Croatia (Guildford: Bradt, 2010)

·Mommsen, Theodor, T. Robert S Broughton, and Theodor Mommsen, The Provinces Of The Roman Empire (Chicago: University of Chicago Press, 1968), p. 203-

·Muljačić, Žarko, "O Dalmatoromanizmima U Marulićevim Djelima", Colloquia Maruliana, 12 (2003), 131-142

·Norton, Peter B., and Robert McHenry, The Encyclopedia Britannica: Macropædia - Knowledge In Depth (Chicago: Encyclopaedia Britannica, Inc., 2003), p. 623

·Rheubottom, David, Age, Marriage, And Politics In Fifteenth-Century Ragusa (Oxford: Oxford University Press, 2000).

·Stipčević, Aleksandar, Iliri (Zagreb: Školska knjiga Zagreb, 1974), p. 70

·Wilkinson, Sir John Gardner, Dalmatia And Montenegro (London: Spottiswoode and Shaw, 1848), p. 274

POETRY

AROUND ISLANDS

BY BRONWEN EVANS

Does the sea know she looks like a person?
You fill my mind with every movement
so together in itself, unified. So free
but with a job to do. To be the whole sea.
Can a dark translucent blue
raised upon a blackened hue
be a someone. Oh yes, to me. This is
the darkest water I have ever seen,
and it holds your long raincoat, your necklaces,
your eyes, and everywhere you've ever been.
Do we become the things we love the most
so that when people find them, all they can see
is us. This way of seeing barely uses eyes,
only to see the sea and know it is there
if you cannot already hear it. Like an extra sense
that remembers, it finds you in an unexplainable
unsurprising way. There you are, of course.
All the familiarities of your being swarm the front
of my thoughts. It is like a dream within which
you know exactly who you are talking to
though they have another's face, but still I am sure,
mind flooded, vision afloat, it can only be
one person. You come to mind with no trying
or thinking, and there is no doubt.
I knew you had left in the forest,
but I found you every night.

LOONEY LOVERS

BY STEPHANIE MARRIE

Let me ask you, Bugs.
Why settle for Elmer Fudd
When you've Daffy Duck?

Don't misunderstand.
It's not about trickery
but equality.

You need a new man.
He needs a new dance partner
and Porky's too slow.

Siegfried and Brunhild
are overrated as heck
and old-fashioned too.

Danny and Dinah
Now there's a fine young couple
scatting saucily.

You'd be a dead-on Dinah
and he was a killer Kaye-
dark eyes, Russian lilt.

Boys trip over
your red lips,
ersatz hips
and mannequin legs.

but could that suit
make you fall
just as hard?

Don't underestimate
what he can do
to a woman.

Even the Morning Glory
bats her eyes at him.

I DID NOT ASK FOR IT

BY H. L. RIVERS

I did not ask for it

When I was asleep in my bed
And he clawed me.
Crawled on top,
Touching me.

I did ask for help,
I did plead with him,
Crying, reasoning, pushing,
But I did not ask for it.

I did not ask for it

When he unhooked my bra
At work. In the daytime.
Covered from neck to toe.

I did not ask him to stop immediately
As he grinded against me
As I stood in shock and fear,
As other people watched
Tears slide down
And still they did nothing.

I did ask for him to stop
When the shock wore off
When I found a voice.
It was quivering and scared
Innocent and abhorred.
He laughed.
I needed to take a joke.

I did not ask for it

When he called me to his office
To discuss my work performance
And his hand went up my thigh.
I did not slap him away
Run away and scream.
I thought maybe I should take this
As a joke too?
So, I laughed. And brushed his hand away,
And left his office full of shame.

I did tell him that I was not interested
I was new and young.
Just getting started.
I had a lot to prove
A lot to do.
But he always found a way
To move in real close and
Slip his hand around my waist,
And whisper in my ear
"Hey, it's okay".
But I did not think it was okay.

I did not ask for it

When another grabbed my shoes
He told me that I had nothing to lose
As he tried to kiss me again,
I pulled loose and said NO.
I did not ask for him to ignore me,
To grab my wrists and hurt me.

I did not ask for it.

LAST EMBRACE (SPOKEN WORD)

BY JITE IMIRUAYE

My mind rested
My heart ablaze
Appearing unfazed;
In a rush, a hurry, skirting to some
Place (I said).
Tried my best to shorten our exchange.
I planned this all before we embraced
But,
I didn't plan that look on your face
dared not look at it.

Hiding beneath your back
The warmth of your body was enough
To resurrect
all of those fuzzy feelings
in all their grotesque forms.
The tingling spread
From your heart to mine,
Slithering down my spine,
 I began to twist out of your clasp
But-
You held me for longer than you naturally would
And I let go quicker than I usually could.

Your arms were wrapped around me for
Two seconds, too long
I felt you, all of you for the first time
 and i still feel your heart throbbing now.
It's etched to mine and I comfortably hate it,
it's comfortable to hate it
to hate you
to hate me

to hate us, to hate, to hate, to hate
and to no longer love.

FORD OF THE LIES

BY AL PINE

In the linguistical intersection
Between demonstrating one's beauty
and admiring the external scenery,
one is left with a lazy eye
for inner detail.
Do our surroundings present us with joy...
Or is our perspective our only toy?
Now, I feel I'm still just a boy
With growing pains amidst all this
Nihilism
of which I've been known to partake
and I've always said
'it's for love's sake'
But then, maybe I've never
Truly been awake!

In crossing the Ford of the Lies,
There is no real diff'rence
Twixt the 'hi's' and 'goodbyes'.

DRUNK ON WONDERLAND

BY MIA PIDLAOAN

I long for the softness of your lips engulfing mine again.
I crave the feeling of your hands holding me close, pressing my head to your chest
The steady heartbeat underneath your warm flesh and bone.

I hope you miss how I stroked your hair,
how I admired the reality of you being next to me as you drove us around,
how I bent and bowed to your pleasure
how I gratefully took everything you offered me.

I miss how your words seemed to spill from your mouth endlessly
As you always had something new and interesting to share
and I would sit there, listening, soaking in the information
More precious facts about you to be tucked away in my mind.

I want to patch all of the holes in your shirts, but moreover
I want to fill the gaping hole you've left in my heart.

I miss your weight on me,
the way you'd abuse my body until you knew I couldn't take any more,
the language of our bodies that you and I picked up naturally
and only grow more fluent in.
I want to speak it more.

I want to hear you play the saxophone more, even more horribly if you can manage it
So when I listen to you play again and again,
I can pick up the notes where you improve from the last time
And I can see you start to regain the remnants of your former self,
the high school you coming back to the surface
Seeing a side of you I'd never get to see otherwise,
having a taste of what the people close to you had in order to satisfy my jealousy

I miss your jovial and sweet aura, infectious and good

You say that you have a strong poker face and monotonous voice
But your wide smile that reached your eyes,
the lilt and kind timbre in your words,
and the walls that came crashing down the moment that we saw each other
said otherwise

After knowing of your existence for eight years
and getting to know you for two days,
I am scared to admit that I may indeed be able to fall in love with someone like you

However

Can I trust those eyes that change colors so often to keep that sweet look
and to never turn dark with hatred towards me one day?
Can I trust those hands that hold me so close and sure to never let me go?
Can I trust the patience and confidence you carry to never falter? Or at the very least, to return after it leaves, as I'm sure it will sometimes?

Can I trust in myself to make a right decision when it comes to love after having failed so many times?

Love, to me, is like Alice falling deep into the rabbit hole
I become disoriented, I can't tell which way is up and which way is down
What are those sounds?
Where am I going?
Who am I truly following?

Can I trust the voice that tells me to stay?
My mind tells me to stay away.

My heart wants to be held, but by whom?
By you or by me?

I'm falling deeper and deeper into this rabbit hole
I fear I won't be able to return to the surface again
Will I regret this?

One thing is for sure.

I am absolutely terrified.

SHORT STORY

DERIVATION

BY TOM LEES

At the end of the world sits a wooden cabin with a stone chimney. Despite the aged and worn exterior of this cabin, it sits comfortably in its place in the world, as though basking in its solitude. The chimney's exterior mimics that of the cabin – of course it does, the two are one in the same and seem to have accompanied one another for millennia, when the world was young... much like the two bedraggled gentlemen occupying this sanctuary.

The first of these gentlemen sits at a desk, writing a book nearing its final pages. His pen dances along the paper, in the comfortable grasp of a trained, fluid wrist. The second gentleman sits in an armchair, comfortably reading a book. Like the men themselves, the book is in a weathered condition – impossibly old, yet unbroken. He reads in candlelight.

Both gentlemen don similar apparel in similar condition. They each wear a black robe that, like them, has withered with time. Perhaps those pairs are the only robes they own. Of course, one set of robes is longer to suit the height of the second gentleman. While the sizes differ, both of their robes show signs of fine golden stitching across the sleeves, with an unknown insignia stitched on where the robes align to their chests. The insignia itself is difficult to see; it is no longer as visible as it was eons ago... but that doesn't matter. Only these two men know what their insignia – their order – represents.

The first gentleman's wrist abruptly pauses, as though time had frozen. He slowly swivels in his battered chesterfield chair to face his friend.

"How many?" he asked calmly. The second gentleman releases an internalised sigh – he must have been invested in his reading. He slowly tilts his head, redirecting his gaze away from the book and towards his friend.

"Must you?" the bookworm asks.

"Yes, unfortunately. The Third Derivation must sing songs of the Second."

The second gentleman pauses for a moment. He forms a frown as though lost in thoughts he'd rather not return to. The candlelight isn't forming demeaning shadows under his eyes – those are his bags, small pockets of age and woe. He swallows.

"All of them," he mutters, "but all I know is that they were lonely."

"All of them?"

"Yes, all of them..." he retorts, bitterly.

After a moment of shared eye contact, the second gentleman returns to the safe space of his book. However, the air has not yet returned to its silent stillness – the other resumes his writing, filling the room with whispers of his penned words.

'So did he... bear witness... to... the Lonely Ones... whose partings... may have otherwise... remained... unremembered.'

The scribe lowers his pen at long last. He releases a sigh of relief and, with it, both the tension and exhaustion his poor wrist has endured performing this delicate dance. He takes a moment to compose himself, eager to recite the words of this final page, and then faces his friend.

'There! May I present?' requests the weary writer. The second gentleman snaps out of the entrancing world of his book. Yes, his reading may be gripping, but as is the excitement of hearing that the tome has finally been complete. Their duties may finally be fulfilled.

'Yes! Enlighten me, friend!' he says as he snaps his book shut, completely disregarding the page he was just reading.

The first gentleman stands. He prepares:

'As the Second Derivation enters its exodus, with two souls waiting at the end times, we leave these writings unto you – the Third Derivation, in the hope that you will hold our lives in the genesis of your memory, when you achieve consciousness. As we scribe these words, we do not know what happens in the end. But we are of the belief that this secret should not be uncovered alone. For this reason, we implore you to anoint two vessels who will continue our duty, after we have reached our resting place. As One sang the songs of the lone dead across space and time for all to rejoice, so did the Other bear witness to the Lonely Ones, whose partings may have otherwise remained unremembered. We ask of whichever two you choose to do the same, as we did in respect of those before us.'

The second gentleman simply sits, startled, like he is in a state of trance or bewilderment. Neither of them can believe their work is now done... but it doesn't take long for concern to get the better of the second gentleman. Their duties may be fulfilled, yes, but now they must beg the question: has everything been done?

"Do you think they will understand?" he asks.

"I hope they will..." the first gentleman replies. The second gentleman's confidence has been knocked slightly. He can feel the uncertainty resonating from his colleague more than he can feel it in himself. To communicate this, he simply raises his thick, sharp eyebrow.

"They will. I am sure." the first gentleman amends. They can't risk leaving any of their lifelong work unfinished. The Third Derivation must know everything.

The first gentleman undergoes a process of binding the book closed. As a means of clearing the air from uncertainty and worry, the two strike up small talk.

"So, where shall you rest now that we have fulfilled our duties?" the first wonders.

"Oh, I don't know. I may just sit in a cave and disintegrate with the sands of time," responds the second, "yourself?"

"Neither. I might let the flames claim my body and let my ashes scatter across the atmosphere, or what remains of it."

"Ah, very elegant."

The first gentleman completes the binding of the book. It is sealed shut with buckle-like locks and rusted chains attached to the spine. He displays the book on a lectern, in hope that members of the Third Derivation will find it and unlock is contents. He turns around to face his seated friend.

"And that's that! We can rest at long last..."

The air of concern returns. As though a ghostly manifestation haunts them both.

"You're concerned..." the first notices.

"And you're not?" retorts the second.

"I am..."

The air is still with silence. They cannot even hear the flickering of the candlelight. The concern begins to mutate into a feeling of realisation; neither of them like this. They have dedicated their lives to their work for so long that they do not know what to do with their emotions. Now is their last chance to reflect.

The second gentleman, restless in his seat, breaks the silence.

"You and I have been here all this time, yet we do not know what happens in the end... has that ever occurred to you?"

His friend takes a moment to ponder. He frowns, indicating that the realisation has grown stronger in him.

"No," he confesses, "though, I suppose we shall find out soon."

Before the silence returns to haunt them any longer, they decide to focus on the lighter side of things – they have both been relieved of their duties, and they can now rest. In its own time, the world will introduce the Third Derivation to existence when it is ready. The second gentleman rises from his seat.

"Whatever happens now, I hope to see you there." bids the second gentleman.

"Likewise!" his dear friend exclaims.

"Goodbye, my friend."

"Farewell."

They both approach the front door of the cabin. For the first time in eons, they shall see sunlight once more before they depart... but a force is stopping them. Their concern did not dissipate – they simply internalised it from one another. Yet they both share an identical worry. Both turn towards the lectern, where the aged, chained book sits before them. It basks in the empowering light of the various candles scattered across the cabin's shelves and mantlepieces. As they turn, the floor lets out a dreary creak – surprising given the age of the cabin. The gentleman thought they would have squeezed every possible noise from this dying sanctuary.

"It's horrible, isn't it?" the second gentleman asks. They both feel the same dread.

"Vile. What is that? Regret? Fear?" wonders the first gentleman.

"A hybrid of the two…" the second gentleman proposes.

Neither of them can cope with the dread they are experiencing. As a means of ending it, the second gentleman promptly grabs the book from the lectern and slams it on the desk. They both hastily undo the locks and free it from its shackles, throwing them on the floor. The coldness of the chains manages to extinguish a few of the candles, both upon impact and from the sheer force of being thrown. The second gentleman flicks through the enormous book, as though he's managing to read entire pages in a matter of milliseconds.

"Stop there!" the first gentleman cries. The second immediately stops flicking. This time, he carefully scans this peculiar page – every name of everyone who ever died alone in the Second Derivation lies catalogued in this book. Yet, their fear was nothing hypothetical. It was real. The gentlemen's eyes widen in shock and dread. Their work is incomplete.

"We have forgotten someone."

BOOK

BY DOAN HAI NGUYEN

A nine-year old Malus got home from school. He planned to go out with his new friend, Poena, but before he could do so, his parents ordered him to join them for a lunch.

"Is this the food we got last week, Mom?" the young boy asked. His mother nodded with a big smile on her face.

"And son, could you finish it, today? We wouldn't it you waste it like the last time," his father demanded.

"Don't be like that on him," his mother said with a frown upside down. "I'm sorry, darling, but what he gets, he eats. All of it."

"I wasn't really hungry at the time, Dad. I was... sad," he muttered.

"Well, don't be, son. Once you grow up into a real man, you'll find out the world is worse than that–" He stopped speaking when he noticed his wife raising her eyebrows. Malus carried on eating without saying anything else for the rest of the lunch.

An hour later, Malus finally finished his meal and headed out to spend some time with Poena. While in the garden, Poena asked the boy about the fading bruise on his arms. However, the blonde boy brushed it off and didn't say anything. Poena scratched his head and gave him a dazed look. Not for the reason his classmate didn't make a deal out of it, but because he casually raised his shoulders as if he faced this question before.

"My parents are just... strict, Poena."

He replied with a lowered tone, "That's alright, Mal. My parents are strict too. Maybe even more..."

A few hours passed by and the boys messed around the house. Poena went to take a leak and during it, Malus' mother came by and asked about her sons' new friend.

"So, how are you two? Are you enjoying each other?"

"Yes! Mom, I think... he might be my new best friend. He's nice and–and looks smart too!" "Oh, sweetie, how many times have I heard that?"

"I mean it this time! He–he's really clever, I think he won't get us into trouble like the other ones..."

"But you know what happens if he does–"

"Yes, I know."

"Alright, then. I hope you're not wrong."

Another hour passed by and the boys goofed around. Both laughed, both danced, having the time of their lives. Their faces grinned in red, and their little hearts beat fast as never before. Both of them eventually stumbled across a door which led to the attic. Poena wanted to go up but Malus refused since they were not allowed to go there.

"Apparently... our–our family's book is in there. But it's sacred, so only my parents and grandparents can look. My dad told me once I get older, I can go see it as well!"

Notwithstanding, this was not enough to stop the rebellious Poena, who always had a way to break the rules no matter what kinds of consequences he faced. Malus sweated and stuttered while Poena encouraged him. He offered him a hand to invite him for their next adventure. "Come on! Live a little."

Eyes filled with terror, lips dried, Malus reached back and both walked to the attic and there it was: the family book. As they headed towards it, Malus' kept looking behind him to expect spanking from his parents. His body shook and despite it was hot outside, he froze.

"We shouldn't be here, Poena!

He didn't listen, he only wished to see the book. And so, he opened it. And what he saw was... horrifying. Pictures of little children--appropriately at the age between seven to nine--in the basement, covered in their own blood. Their faces swollen, and their bodies mutilated until nothing but raw flesh stayed. Next to those were clips from newspapers, talking about the children's whereabouts. Poena's face became green, his lips shook, and his eyes filled with tears. Seconds later, he threw up on the floor, and made his white face even more pale.

This moment scarred young Poena on the soul, but what he didn't notice at first were the adults in those pictures. When he did, chills went down his spine. It was them... and it was too late.

"I told you, we shouldn't be here," Malus said with a neutral expression before he wrapped his hands around his classmate's neck and pushed him down the stairs, knocking him out. Moments later, the whole familytook a stand around their new victimbefore trapping him in the basement.

"Well, there goes your next lunch, son," the father sighed.

"Oh, sweetie, why is it always so hard for you to find good-behaved friends? I told you not to invite him in until... you know..." the mother shook her head.

"I'm sorry, Mom. I just... wanted a friend. I didn't know he would not listen to me... he really seemed smart" the boy defended himself.

"Fucking hell, like I haven't taught you anything or what?!" the father shouted before his wife dragged him away. The two of them left their son standing at the door, watching his unconscious classmate--someone, who would become yet another of their many victims. Their son needed a moment to comprehend their situation once again.

"You should have listened to me, Poena. Children should always be obedient. But... it seems your parents haven't taught you that enough," Malus uttered his last words to Poena before closing the door, cutting him off from his life forever. Sometimes, "living a little" only brought the worst in people.

NEW NATION DISCOVERED

BY AL PINE

"Good evening ladies and gentlemen, you're listening to the news.

"New Nation Discovered, or elaborate Internet hoax?

"The meteorological world was sent into a frenzy earlier today when several weather satellite images appeared to reveal the existence of an enormous landmass located in the South East Pacific Ocean. The landmass seemed to appear on regional shipping weather reports early yesterday morning and remained on them throughout the day, in one of the most remote regions of Earth. The images suggested that the landmass was roughly the size of Scandinavia, and in several areas even showed some signs of human habitation in the form of artificial lighting after dark. The landmass has since disappeared again as suddenly as it came.

"The World Meteorological Organization has as yet given no account for the phenomenon; the most likely explanation seems to be mischievous hackers playing some sort of prank with the world's weather satellite systems. A spokesperson did assure us earlier, however, that if such a landmass had been in evidence yesterday, it did not seem to have hindered the progress of the more than forty cruise ships and cargo vessels sailing through the area in question. All the ships have been reporting normal sailing conditions.

"In other news, hippies and new-agers the world over took part yesterday in World Meditation Day. Research suggests that an average of over 8000 tree-huggers, sandal-wearers, lentil-munchers, incense-burners and practitioners of an 'alternative' lifestyle in each time zone attended pre-arranged locations for a twenty-minute meditation in the hope of 'raising the conscious frequency of the noosphere', as one spokeswoman for the movement in Australia put it. The woman, who goes by the curious name of 'Outside The System', is hoping for World Meditation Day to become a monthly phenomenon..."

***

Four weeks later

Flight Commander P. R. Johnson was a man who followed his orders unquestioningly, no matter how bizarre they were. He had been given a most nonsensical reconnaissance mission by the Pentagon to fly in a big circle around the South East Pacific and "report back any sightings of unidentified land"; and that was exactly what he and his squadron were doing.

"Ain't it all just so wide and blue and boring as ever, sir," one of his wingmen, Flight Lieutenant Newgear, quipped over the comlink.

"Would ya rather have stayed on the ground?" Johnson retorted.

"Nah, course not. But it makes ya wonder, don't it, sir?"

Johnson flew on for a moment in silence. "Nope," he concluded finally. Then, after another long moment, more to relieve the monotony of staring at hundreds more miles of featureless azure ocean than out of any real sense of curiosity, he added: "Wonder what, exactly?"

"What the point of this is, sir."

"We're doin' it because we've been ordered to do it. That's good enough for me, and it better be good enough for you too."

"Yes, sir. It sure is, sir. But, I dunno...you must've heard about that freaky incident with the weather station and the South Pacific landmass a few weeks back?"

Johnson sighed. "Who hasn't?"

"Well, looks to me like the Pentagon must be takin' the whole thing kinda seriously. I reckon they sure ain't sendin' us up here for shits and giggles, sir."

"Flight Lieutenant Newgear, someday your inquisitive nature is gonna land you in a whole heap of trouble."

"I read on the Internet that it wasn't just the weather stations that took pictures of the landmass," Mundy, another member of the squadron, chipped in. "They're saying that all the spy satellites did too, and that if it was a hack-job like they said on the news, the hackers must have been able to get into the highest security clearance."

Newgear whistled. "That's a helluva risk to take for a practical joke," he mused.

"You believe every two-bit conspiracy theory you read on the Internet? Never had you down as that stoopid, Mundy," Flight Commander Johnson said disapprovingly.

"Sir, why else would they be sending us on a reconnaissance mission to this neck of the woods to look for unidentified land? All I can see is several hundred miles of sun-kissed Pacific Ocean."

"Shut up and fly," suggested Flight Commander P. R. Johnson.

**

Jeanette Donnelly, a blogger of some repute in certain esoteric circles, had arranged to meet Amaro and his granddaughter Tica (who had first contacted Jeanette and who spoke excellent English) in a smoky bar in some remote fishing village on the Peruvian south coast.

The weatherbeaten old fisherman spoke slowly, calmly and matter-of-factly in Peruvian Coast Spanish; however the translated words coming from his beautiful granddaughter seemed to belie his offhand manner.

"Yes, my grandfather says he has ever been surprised the weather satellites never picked up the –," Tica paused as if searching for the right word, "– Sometimes Country before."

"The Sometimes Country?" Jeanette prompted.

"Yes. I really cannot translate it any better. The word is not from Spanish, but comes from an indiginous tale far older than the Nazca even, almost completely forgotten until grandfather and others' recent sightings, er – what is the word? Resurrected the myth. I cannot tell the tales of the time before the Nazca ... but the word that translates to Sometimes Country has started to be used again by the fishermen like my grandfather."

Amaro placed a calloused and grizzled hand over Tica's, and said something to her quietly and distinctly.

"He says he and two others have seen the Sometimes Country three times in the last three years whilst far out to sea in his boat, but the rest of his fellow fishermen have not. It is the subject of much amusement here."

Amaro continued to speak to his granddaughter, but his kind eyes – set in deep trenches of wrinkles and crow's feet – regarded Jeanette earnestly and with a peculiar sadness.

"He is explaining that it has been noticed among his brother fishermen, that he and the two others who sail with him and claim to have seen the Sometimes Country are the gentle ones, those in the community slowest to anger and...of the most peaceful nature. The ones who spare the dolphins." Tica broke off, looking uncomfortable. Her eyes swept furtively for a moment around the quiet bar. "Others have been known to use dolphin meat as cost-free bait for shark fishing," she explained bitterly.

Jeanette, who had worked with dolphins when she was younger, made a mental note to look into this further; however she refused to be distracted from the old fisherman's story. "Could he please tell me exactly what he saw?"

"Each time was in broad daylight and very clear visibility," Tica translated Amaro's words after a moment. "Around midafternoon. We were at least three hundred kilometres west of the coastline where Peru meets Chile. No land there, as everyone knows. Just the deep, wide, endless ocean. I have sailed these waters for sixty years and more. The first time we spotted land, he says, it was from a distance. We argued about what we had seen. When we decided to sail the boat closer to investigate, we found nothing.

"The second time, it seemed to appear out of nowhere, no mistake this time. So close that we could make out cliffs and a beach. I and my shipmates had been singing, the sight of land took us by surprise and we were afraid. We sailed away, back in the direction of home."

The old fisherman's voice, always soft, sank now to a whisper. "The third time was just last month," Tica translated. "We were in a philosophical frame of mind, trying to cheer ourselves up after finding no anchovies, when suddenly we noticed several dolphins swimming and jumping some distance in front of our boat. This is very unusual, as they have learned to be wary of our boats in these waters, to my great sadness and shame. We sailed closer and they put on the most splendid show of synchronised jumping. Then they stopped and swam further away before carrying on with their display, as if they wanted us to follow, which we did. This happened three or four times until again ... we could see land before us. Now, we had agreed between us after the last time that if we were ever to see the Sometimes Country again, we would not sail away in fear but would go to investigate. And so we headed for the coast before us – which was as wide as the horizon we could see, north to south – yet we couldn't get any closer." Tica paused as old Amaro lit himself a cigar.

 "We sailed and sailed, but the Sometimes Country grew no closer. The dolphins escorting our boat started singing, not just the usual sounds, but in the most exquisite harmonies with each other. The most exquisite harmonies ... but we couldn't get any closer. Eventually they gave up and swam off, and the Sometimes Country faded into the horizon."

Tica fell silent as the old man came to the end of his story.

***

On board the cruise ship The Frosch Prince, two dozen men and women sat in a heavily curtained, onboard conference room densely scented with sandalwood and liberally scattered with crystals of varying hues upon intricately decorated cloths of rough silk and crushed velvet.

"Guys and gals, you should all give yourselves a pat on the back," Sysi Delmuria told her enraptured audience with that adorable dimpled smile of hers. "Last month's World Meditation was a real breakthrough, as you all know. For the first time, we got over eight and a half thousand people meditating in one location in at least twelve of the twenty-four International Time Zones. As I'm sure I don't need to explain to most of you, 8500 is a very critical number as it represents roughly the square root of one per cent of the global population, in accordance with the Maharishi Effect." Sysi broke off for a moment, treating all her listeners to a fractional moment of eye contact. "As a result of this breakthrough," she continued in a near whisper, "as you all know, a large fissure appeared in the veil between worlds ..."

It was pretty obvious that most of the guys in the CHEG (Conscious Human Evolution Group) were in love with Sysi Delmuria (who, as far as the authorities were concerned, insisted on going by her formal name "Outside The System"), and most of the girls wanted to be her. Petite and perfectly formed, with lustrous chestnut hair and a flawlessly angelic face, she was also searingly keen-witted, impossibly self-assured, and somehow managed to conduct herself in a manner which was both aloof and approachable all at the same time.

"You've all read about the New Landmass Conspiracy," Sysi went on. "As you all know, the sighting of this landmass here in the South East Pacific by at least forty-two weather satellites and who knows how many military satellites worldwide is being passed off as nothing more than an elaborate hoax by mischeivous hackers."

"It has to have been a hoax," one of the more skeptical members of her audience piped up. "I was just talking with this ship's First Officer earlier. This ship is actually due to be sailing through the area in question right about now."

Sysi smiled, her bright green exes flashing in amusement. "What a fool I must have been, to have booked this conference hall, at this time, on a cruise ship scheduled to sail right past the coast of ... my homeland." Slowly, sensuously, she glided across the room to the heavy curtain that shielded the room from the outside glare of the South Pacific sun, and twitched it aside.

Contact us

You can contact Hermes Magazine in these ways.

Email:
Hermesmagazinelondon@yahoo.com

LinkedIn:
www.linkedin.com/company/hermesmagazine

Website:
www.hermesmagazine.yolasite.com

Instagram:
www.instagram.com/hermesmagazinelondon

www.ingramcontent.com/pod-product-compliance
Lightning Source LLC
LaVergne TN
LVHW080042090426

835510LV00042B/1936